Real Estate Investment Strategy

The Ultimate Beginner's Guide to Real Estate Investing

© Copyright 2019 - All rights reserved.

The content contained within this book may not be reproduced, duplicated, or transmitted without direct written permission from the author or the publisher.

Under no circumstances will any blame or legal responsibility be held against the publisher, or author, for any damages, reparation, or monetary loss due to the information contained within this book. Either directly or indirectly.

Legal Notice:
This book is copyright protected. This book is only for personal use. You cannot amend, distribute, sell, use, quote or paraphrase any part, or the content within this book, without the consent of the author or publisher.

Disclaimer Notice:
Please note the information contained within this document is for educational and entertainment purposes only. All effort has been executed to present accurate, up to date, and reliable, complete information. No warranties of any kind are declared or implied. Readers acknowledge that the author is not engaging in the rendering of legal, financial, medical, or professional advice. The content within this book has been derived from various sources. Please consult a licensed professional before attempting any techniques outlined in this book.

By reading this document, the reader agrees that under no circumstances is the author responsible for any losses, direct or indirect, which are incurred as a result of the use of the information contained within this document, including, but not limited to, — errors, omissions, or inaccuracies.

Table of Contents

Introduction 1

Chapter 1: What Is Real Estate Investment? 3

Real Estate Investing: What Does It Mean? 4

The Real Estate Sector: How Does It Work? 5
- Economy 5
- Demographics 6
- Interest Rates 6

Understanding the Real Estate Market 7
- Know the Market 7
- Get Adequate Investment Capital 8
- Keep Up With the Real Estate Laws 9

Benefits of Investing In Real Estate 12
- A Broad Range of Options 12
- It Lets You Make Money on the Side 12
- Protected Against Inflation 13
- You Don't Need Comprehensive Education 13
- Tangible Assets 13
- There is Not a lot of Risk Involved 14
- Numerous Options for Financing 14
- You Earn Passive Income 15
- It Lets You Build Your Investment Portfolio 15
- It Provides a Continuous Stream of Income 16
- It Appreciates 16
- You are Responsible for Your Choices 16
- Exemption from Taxes 17
- You Don't Have to Pay Your Mortgage Yourself 17

Drawbacks of Investing in Real Estate 18
- Legal Issues 18
- Your Properties Will Require Maintenance 18
- There is No Liquidity 19
- It Needs a lot of Time 19
- There May be Inefficiencies in Real Estate 19

Is Real Estate Better Than Other Forms of Investments?..20

The Three Major Methods of Investing in Real Estate 21

Chapter 2: Types of Real Estate Properties to Invest In 22

Agricultural Properties 22

Residential Properties 23

Commercial Properties 26

Industrial Properties 27
- Mixed-Use...27
- Special Purpose Property..28

Chapter 3: Individuals You Should Buy Properties From 29
- Buying from Owners with Equity......................................29
- Purchasing from Owners without Equity 30
- Buying Foreclosed Homes at Auctions 31
- Buying Foreclosures Owned by a Bank.............................32
- Purchasing from Absentee Owners with Equity...............33

Which is the Best One for You? 33
- Your Time Frame 33
- Your Nature 34
- Your Location 34

Chapter 4: Locating The Best Real Estate Investment Deals 35
- Check the Local Newspaper..35
- Checkout Pocket Listings..36
- Word of Mouth 36
- Direct Mail 37
- Drive Around Neighborhoods 37
- Use Cold Calls...38
- Try Property Management Corporations.........................38
- Eviction Courts..39
- Connect with a Title Company 39
- Try Apartment or Landlord Association Meetings..........40

Real Estate Investing Meetings 40
Tax Delinquencies 41
Multiple Listing Service (MLS) 41
Vendors 41
Social Media 42
Real Estate Attorneys 42

Ensuring You Profit after Your Investment 43

Chapter 5: Getting Real Estate Investment Finance ... 44

Real Estate Loans: Important Things to Understand 44

Get a Correct Estimate of the Amount You Will Need for Renovating the Property 46
Build Your Network 46

Best Sources of Financing 47

Get Loans from Family or Friends 47
Tap into Your 401(k) 48
Use Personal Loans 49
Find Yourself a Financing Partner 50
A Business Line of Credit 51
Home Equity Loan (HEL) 52
Real Estate Crowdfunding 53
Seller Financing 53
Small Business Association Loans (SBA) 55
Hard Money Loans 56
Collaborate with a Mortgage Broker 57

Choosing the Best Option 58

Chapter 6: Putting Your Real Estate Team Together . 59

How Does a Real Estate Investment Team Help You? 59

Professionals to Include in Your Team 60

Real Estate Agents 60
Contractors 62
Appraisers and Inspectors 64
Wholesalers 65
Lenders 66
Bookkeepers 66

- CPA (Certified Public Accountant) 67
- Lawyers 67
- Property Managers 67
- General Handyman 68
- Pest Control Company 68
- Insurance Broker 69

When Should You Build Your Team? 69

Where to Find Your Real Estate Investing Team 70

Chapter 7: Wholesaling Real Estate 71

Benefits of Being a Wholesale Investor 72

Drawbacks to Being a Wholesale Investor 72

Steps Involved in Wholesaling Real Estate 73
- Do Your Research 73
- Develop a Buyer's List 73
- Market to Sellers with the Desire to Sell 74
- Get a Property Under Contract 74
- Locate Your End Buyer 75
- Get the Contract Assigned 76
- Close the Deal 76

How to Know if Wholesaling a Property is Ideal for You 77

Calculating your Wholesale Profit 78

Chapter 8: Fix and Flip/Home Rehab 80

Home Rehab: What is it? 81

Advantages of Flipping Properties 82

Drawbacks of Flipping Properties 83

Steps in Home Rehabbing 84
- Do Your Research 84
- Develop Your Business Plan and Budget 84
- Get Financing in Advance 85
- Find the Right Contractors 85
- Locate a Property to Flip 86
- Purchase the Property 87

Rehab 87
Sell the Property 88

Chapter 9: Rental Property Investment 90

Rental Real Estate: What Is It? 90

Benefits of Investing in Rentals 91

Drawbacks of Investing in Rentals 92

How to Invest in Rental Properties 93
Do Comprehensive Research Before You Buy 93
Create a Plan 94
Get Your Finances in Order 94
Begin Your Search for a Rental Property You Can Buy 95
Make the Seller an Offer 96
Do Your Due Diligence 97

Getting the Services of a Property Manager 98

Is Investing in Rental Properties a Wise Decision?. 99

Chapter 10: Making Offers in Real Estate 100
Develop an Amazing Offer 100
Run an Analysis of the Market 100
Monitor Market Indicators 101
Determine the Motivation of the Seller 102
Find out About the Other Offers on the Property 102
Apply for a Pre-approval Letter 103
Make a Larger Downpayment 104
Let an Attorney Evaluate Your Offer 104

Engaging in Negotiations 104
Bidding Strategies 105
Sealed bids 106
Holding Deposits 106

Seller Counteroffers and Responses 107

Chapter 10: Doing Your Due Diligence 109

Tasks Involved in Due Diligence 109
Do Your Research 109
Do a Title Search 111
Follow the Homeowner's Association Requirements 111

Doing a Property Inspection 112
Making Preparations for a Property Inspection 113
Things Home Inspection Might Not Cover 115

Things to Inspect on a Property 116
Inspection for Wood-destroying Organisms (WDO) 116
Radon Gas Inspection 117
Lead-based Paint Inspection 117

The Final Step: Run Your Numbers 118
What Should You Do When the Numbers Are Not Right? 118

Chapter 11: Common Real Estate Misconceptions ... 120
Making Money in Real Estate is Very Easy 120
The Best Place to Buy Real Estate is Downtown 121
You Need a Ton of Money to Start the Business 121
Investing in Real Estate Requires you to Have a License 122
Tenants Leave When Rent is Increased 123
You Can Earn Passively by Investing in Real Estate 123
You Should be a Homeowner Before Investing in Rental Properties . 124
You Must Always Make a Huge Profit 124
Your Investment Should be Close to Where You Live 124
You Need to Have Connections to Invest 125
You Need Luck to Make a Substantial Profit 125
You Can Make Money While You Sleep Once You Own Lots of Properties 125

Conclusion 126

Introduction

At some point, you may have come across the term "Real Estate Investment." It is not a new term and for many investors around the globe, it is one of the most widespread means of investing. It is a very easy and profitable means to earn short and long-term income depending on which option you go with. Even if you have had no personal dealings with real estate, you most likely know someone who is making it big time. Or perhaps you have seen one of those shows where properties are fixed up and sold for a much higher price. All of these have piqued your interest, and now you too want to take a bite from this huge market.

But, you have a major problem: you know nothing about investing in real estate, and you are probably asking yourself *"How do I start?" How do I get the financing? Where can I buy properties?"* These and many more are some of the things I will be sharing with you in this book.

Over the years, I have invested in numerous properties and turned them for profit. In real estate, you pick up some lessons, and learn from your mistakes. But, in this book, I will be saving you from the stress of making mistakes and showing you the steps that worked for me. The information I will be sharing in this book are things I picked up from my first-hand real estate experience. You are going to be hearing directly from the horse's mouth many of the things that can ensure your journey into real estate is a seamless one.

I have shared this strategy with tons of people and they have all come back to tell me how well it worked for them. You don't have to be left out, as these strategies can work well for you as well. You have already taken a good first step by purchasing this book, and as we go further you will be learning all of the important things you need to know about real estate investing.

We will begin from the basics and get down to the complex aspects like getting finance for your project. You will also learn how to make offers, and the types of properties you can invest in. Furthermore, we will look into some of the misconceptions that have made many prospective investors back out of real estate or even invest wrongly. These myths and many more will be uncovered in this book.

Now, let's get started on this journey to make you an amazing real estate investor.

Chapter 1: What Is Real Estate Investment?

When it comes to real estate investment, the aim is to invest your cash so that it works for you, and hold on to property until the value increases in the future. If you invest in a property like this, the returns you get must be adequate to cover all of the additional risks. These span from paid taxes, to cost of maintenance, insurance, and utilities, among others, all of which come with owning property.

If you have proper knowledge of the economics and risks behind investing in real estate, the venture can be a simple and profitable one. To earn more, you can even invest in even more properties. But, you need to remember that even though real estate investment is a simple method of investing, the process is not quite so straightforward. In real estate, mistakes can be dire, and doing something the wrong way could result in you spending massive amounts on legal fees and damages. In the worst instances, you could end up bankrupt and broke.

All of these make it necessary for you to arm yourself with proper knowledge of investing in real estate. These include the types of properties to invest in, and the benefits and drawbacks of investing in real estate. All of these and much more are some of the areas we will be looking into in this chapter. First, let's delve a little into what real estate investment means.

Real Estate Investing: What Does It Mean?

Real estate investing refers to a diverse category of managing, investment, and every financial activity that involves earning money from tangible properties. However, it does not stop there, as real estate equally consists of all of the cash flow that is linked with physical properties.

Your options of earning cash in real estate are limitless, and below are a few of them:

- **Rise of Real Estate**: In this situation, there is an increase in a property's value. This may be due to a change in the real estate market, which results in a rise in demand for properties in the area your investment property is situated. The reason may be due to the upgrades you have made on the property, or a rise in the appeal of the neighborhood. All of these can make properties more attractive to prospective buyers.

- **Real Estate Income:** These include the earnings agents alongside other real estate professionals get as commission from selling or purchasing properties. These also include companies which manage real estate and earn a part of the rent, or all of it, in exchange for the service of running the daily operations of a property.

- **Rent**: Here, you buy a real estate building and manage it as opposed to selling it to get earnings in the form of rent.

We will be taking a more detailed look at this in the chapters to come.

- **Earnings from Ancillary Real Estate Investment**: This is the money you make from items in your real estate investment property like vending machines in office buildings or apartments, or laundry facilities. These consist of all other kinds of smaller businesses you can locate in much more significant real estate investments, which let you make even more money from a smaller portion of individuals.

The Real Estate Sector: How Does It Work?

Real estate also includes the establishment, development, and the sale of real estate. It has a considerable effect on the United States economy because it is a core driving force for the development of the economy. Furthermore, real estate is categorized by country, state, and market condition, which undergoes changes due to a range of factors we will cover below.

Economy

A prosperous economy has an effect on the real estate market. When the economy is healthy, the real estate market becomes healthy, too. During periods when people spend a tremendous amount of cash as consumers, it means they are in a better position to purchase real estate. The more people buy homes, the more demand there is, which then leads to an increase in property value. The reverse is applicable when the economy is in terrible shape. In this situation, there will be more instances of foreclosure, and not as many people will have the capacity to purchase a property. Due to this, properties may stay longer than necessary on the market, which will result in a reduction in their prices.

Demographics

Age, family status, and income all have a role to play in determining property value in a specific region. A city which has lots of parks and educational facilities will be more appealing to families, while one with lots of industries will be appealing to business experts and professionals. The people and the income of those purchasing properties in a precise area can be a significant determinant of the real estate market in that neighborhood.

Interest Rates

Each day, the rates of interest on mortgages change. During the periods when interest is high, people will have less capacity to purchase properties. Some individuals wait till the prices go back down, while others won't have the means to finance a mortgage payment with high interest. If the interest rates go up drastically, it can have a noticeable effect on the market for real estate, and in worse instances, it can put the market on hold until there is a rise in interest once more. If you are quoted a low rate of interest when you are purchasing a property, you can ask that your lender locks in the rate. Doing this will make sure that the prices cannot be altered during the process of underwriting your loan.

Having covered these, we will cover a few things you need to know to start investing in real estate if you want to make real money in the next section.

Understanding the Real Estate Market

Know the Market

- **Property values**: To know if you are getting an excellent deal on a property, you need knowledge of the present cost of properties in your neighborhood. You can either get a licensed real estate agent to help you out with this or get licensed. This way, you can gain access to listing prices.

- **Know the value of rent**: If your goal is to invest in rental properties, you need knowledge of the typical amount of rents in your neighborhood. If you want to be a smart investor, you need to understand the earning potential of your property. A great way of knowing this is to learn the amount of rent that will come in. This is possible by getting a professional appraiser to help you out.

- **Don't overspend**: When purchasing a home to live in, you can invest as much cash as you want without any hassles. However, when it has to do with investment, you need the best prices on the market, or even below market prices. It will be vital regardless of the investment route you decide to take.

Get Adequate Investment Capital

Like we have stated earlier, real estate is a venture that requires cash. This means you will need to push in more cash into a transaction in contrast to when you are purchasing a home to reside in. Below are a few reasons for this:

- **You need no less than a 20% downpayment**: For properties you want to invest in, you will need a downpayment of no less than 20% of the cost of purchase. Depending on the seller, and the kind of investment property, there are instances when this downpayment is much higher.

- **Unforeseen Repairs might arise**: If you are looking to purchase properties below market value, there is a huge possibility that some will be in bad shape. To get them up to standard, you will require a lot of cash. This will have a lot of impact on how fast you can rent or flip the property. For this reason, you need to have a good amount of cash in place.

- **Off-peak periods**: Many investors fail to prepare for this. However, as a real estate investor, you need to note that there are periods where you won't get any income from rent. This is the case when you are stuck with a terrible tenant who refuses to pay, or an instance when tenants sneak out and leave before payment. It is vital for you to have an adequate amount of money in place if the money trickling in from rent stops unexpectedly. This way, you can keep yourself afloat until you get things in order once more.

- **You may need to do some repairs when switching tenants**: You need cash in place to fix a few things when switching tenants. Regardless of whether you like it or not, the truth remains that most tenants never leave a property the same way they found it. For some, it could be a minor repair like changing a broken mirror or just cleaning up the home. For others, it could be much worse, like fixing appliances and damaged walls.

Keep Up With the Real Estate Laws

As an investor in real estate, you need to take note of all the laws regarding ownership of properties or tenant-landlord relationships.

Below are a few of them:

- **The process of eviction**: Even if you are stuck with a frustrating tenant who refuses to pay their rent, the law still needs you to provide a specific period of notice before eviction. In most instances, this is not less than 30 days. In many states, tenants have the capacity to request a stay of execution, which is typical when there are little kids involved. You need to understand these laws so you don't end up in a legal hassle for breaking rules you never knew existed.

- **Run background checks on potential tenants**: It is best to prevent issues when you can, instead of having them come up when you least expect. Running a proper background check on people you are about to let in your home can save you lots of legal stress and money. You can do a criminal background check and credit check on all of your prospective tenants.

- **Rent security deposits:** When it involves rent security deposits, every region of the country has different processes. In many areas, a standard security deposit is the same as a month's rent alongside the rent for the first month when you have moved in. Find out the practice of the region you are in and stick with it. Don't fall for empty promises made by tenants to forgo this requirement. It is there for your best interest.

- **Insurance**: As a homeowner, your insurance is not the same as when you are an investor. As an investor, you will be required to have coverage against possible injury to individuals who rent your property. General liability insurance coverage may also be a great option in the event one of your tenants or their visitors suffers an injury on your property and slams you with a lawsuit. All of these will ensure you are fully protected and covered from any damages that may arise.

- **The real estate market is never the same for a long time**. It goes through constant change, and no housing environment does not go through a form of change after a while. It may be difficult to predict the incoming change in trends. Then again, by understanding the factors we have covered above, you can at least make a calculated guess. Nonetheless, you need to keep track of the strong points of the market in your neighborhood so that you can determine the value of your property. A way of doing this with ease is to get the help of a licensed agent in the area. Real estate investment can come with a lot of fantastic returns if you are smart about how and where you invest. Knowing this, let's take a look at some of the benefits you stand to gain from investing in real estate.

Benefits of Investing In Real Estate

There are a range of benefits that investing in real estate brings you. Below are some of the major ones:

A Broad Range of Options

When it comes to real estate, one of the main benefits is the limitless opportunities that come with it. There are a range of ways to invest in real estate, which include wholesaling, rental properties, fix and flip, and buy and hold. It also allows for you to pick from various locations and various kinds of properties which we will further examine later in this book. No matter the amount of capital you invest in the venture, and your expected returns, real estate offers you numerous options to meet your requirements and expectations.

It Lets You Make Money on the Side

If you still want to work a full-time job while earning money on the side by investing in real estate, it is possible. This is how a range of individuals in the venture make money from it. As a starter, going part-time into the venture can help you test the waters, while your current job provides you with the finances you require. When you have gotten the hang of it, then you can start to do the business full-time.

Protected Against Inflation

Real estate investing is a venture that is safeguarded against inflation. If you choose to rent your property, you will be able to alter prices based on what the present market allows. This means that regardless of what the market is dealing with, you continue making your money as a landlord. Ultimately, in the long run, any cash you invest in real estate is safeguarded at all times.

You Don't Need Comprehensive Education

To get into the business of real estate investing, you don't have to obtain a specific degree. There are numerous guides and resources online that can easily help you begin alongside this book. What's more, you can build your experience as you go on. The business of real estate lets you learn on the move, which means with time, you can enhance your performance and your knowledge of the business.

Tangible Assets

Investing in real estate lets you have tangible assets. This means you can physically touch and feel the property you are investing all of your money in. This makes it different from other forms of investments that you can't see or touch all through the investment period. This makes it a less scary business venture any individual can engage in.

There is Not a lot of Risk Involved

After the ROI, another area many individuals weigh before investing their money in any business is the level of risk that comes with it. Real estate does not come with a high level of risk; it is a low-risk investment, which makes it worthwhile. The reason is that you are purchasing assets that you can see and touch, which you can insure to make sure you don't lose your investment. The physical property or its monetary value will always be yours. Also, even during the periods of instability in the real estate market, you can still hold on to your investment until it is back to normal again. If you are in luck, you will be able to make more than you anticipated from your investment.

Numerous Options for Financing

Many people who are not very conversant with real estate believe that without a lot of money in your pockets, it is not a venture to go into. This is true to a reasonable extent, but it is not entirely true. Yes, you do require money to push into the business, nevertheless the money does not have to come from your pockets. Real estate provides investors with numerous options to alter their available budget. If you purchase a rental property, you can make a down payment of 20%, and get a mortgage loan to cover the price left. Even if you are not eligible for a mortgage, there are numerous hard money and private money lenders that will grant you the funds you need without excess requirements.

If you go into a partnership or find a finance partner, you can begin without having to invest too much of your funds. The range of options makes it easy to venture into and provides investors with immense benefits.

You Earn Passive Income

To date, passive income remains a better way to earn income, as opposed to active income. This is because it lets you make money even without actively working. A great way of doing this is to invest in a REIT, which operates the way stocks do. Another alternative is to hire a property management service to help with the management of your rental properties. This way, you earn passive income while engaging in other pleasurable activities or working a full-time job.

It Lets You Build Your Investment Portfolio

The goal of many investors is to develop their investment portfolio as quickly as they can. However, this is usually not possible when it comes to typical forms of investment. In contrast, real estate properties give you the chance to do this. With the money you get from rent, you can purchase another property. Better still, you can tap into the equity of one of your properties to buy another property. This way, you keep growing your investment portfolio and earning more as you go further.

It Provides a Continuous Stream of Income

As an investor, your goal is to make money continuously. Then again, many investment opportunities are unable to provide you with instant and constant income. Real estate properties divert from the norm and give you the chance to do it. The instant you purchase a rental property, you can immediately get tenants and start to earn cash from it. So long as you can keep finding suitable tenants, you will keep getting income from rent each month without fail.

It Appreciates

Real estate properties tend to appreciate in the long run. This is particularly the case when you purchase a property in a fast-rising neighborhood. With time, the value of the property will go up, regardless of the changing markets. This means whenever you choose to dispose of your property, you will be getting much more than you initially purchased it for, which translates to extra cash in your pockets.

You are Responsible for Your Choices

As a real estate investor, you do as you please, and report to no one. You have complete control over how you invest and your profits and losses. You are solely responsible for determining the property you wish to channel your resources into, the kind of tenants you want, the members of your team, and how much you want for rent. If you are looking to be your own boss, real estate investing is the way to go.

Exemption from Taxes

As one who invests in real estate, there are many tax exemptions you can enjoy. Investors are exempted from paying taxes when they rent out their property. You are not categorized as self-employed when you earn income from rent, and as such, not meant to pay self-employment tax. What's more, investors are provided with advantageous tax treatments for legal fees, insurance, maintenance repairs, property taxes, and so on. Even when it comes to long-term investments, the same also applies.

You Don't Have to Pay Your Mortgage Yourself

Another great benefit of investing in real estate is that you don't need to be responsible for paying your mortgage. If you have tenants, they can do it for you! This is possible with the money you get from rental income each month, which will be adequate in covering your mortgage payment among other expenses. Ensure your tenants stay happy, and you won't have to face the problem of vacant buildings for an extended period.

Drawbacks of Investing in Real Estate

All investments have their disadvantages, and real estate investment is no different. There is a range of limitations which come with real estate. These limitations include:

Legal Issues

Dealing with a lawsuit can dip into your funds as well as your profit. There are instances where a tenant gets injured on your property and decides to slam you with a lawsuit. This can do a number on your wallet, especially if you have no insurance. In other instances, investors have discovered that the property they purchased had a false title when requesting a loan. This could lead to a rise in legal issues and distress to investors.

Your Properties Will Require Maintenance

Purchasing real estate properties is only the first step. There are instances when you may need to do some maintenance after purchase. In critical situations, this may cost you a considerable amount of funds, while it may be minor in other cases. Additionally, the longer you hold on to a property, the more maintenance costs you will need to pay during this period. Even when you lend out your property for rent, you will still have to invest a lot more cash in maintenance to ensure it remains suitable for living.

There is No Liquidity

This is one core drawback of being a real estate investor. It can be a hassle to liquefy your assets to cash quickly, and from cash back to assets. In other forms of investments like bonds or stocks, this is something you can achieve in a matter of minutes, sometimes seconds. But when it comes to real estate, this process can take months. Even if you get help from a broker, it may be difficult for you to get the right equivalent and may take some weeks.

It Needs a lot of Time

Selling or giving out a property for rent requires a lot of time. This can be a hassle if you work a full-time job elsewhere. You can counter this with ease by getting the services of an expert to oversee and manage things in your absence, but you will need to spend a little extra.

There May be Inefficiencies in Real Estate

There are instances where investors may need to purchase properties without seeing them. This could be through auctions, and in some cases, investors buy properties based on information. They are unable to tell if the deal is a good or bad one until they have paid for the property in full. This can leave them with a lot of unforeseen expenses that bite into their profits.

The same applies to rental properties which have changing demographics that can also dip into the profit. Real estate investing has to do with handling the inefficiencies in the market, which if not handled properly, can lead to substantial financial damages.

Is Real Estate Better Than Other Forms of Investments?

You may have wondered if there are better options for investment other than real estate. The simple answer to this is yes! Even though other forms of investments like bonds, stocks, and certificates of deposit also offer benefits, real estate provides something the others are not able to. This is consistent cash flow which you have direct control and influence over. Your net income is solely dependent on your actions, and no one else. Other kinds of investments are utterly reliant on the company and its officers. In contrast to this, investors are in control of every asset they own, which makes it a much better option than many other forms of investments.

The Three Major Methods of Investing in Real Estate

When considering investing in real estate, the following are the three ways you can get started:

- Wholesale
- Buy and Hold
- Rehab

We will be delving further into these methods of investments in the chapters to come. Even after you have understood all of the real estate investment basics, your task is still incomplete. You still need to have knowledge of the types of real estate properties you can invest in, which we will cover in the following chapter.

Chapter 2: Types of Real Estate Properties to Invest In

Understanding the property options available to you as a real estate investor is another crucial area you need to cover. By learning the various types of properties in real estate, you will be able to find out what works for you, and which can get you the best returns.

There are tons of properties in real estate, all of which investors can get distinct benefits from. In this chapter, we will be looking into some of the significant options.

Agricultural Properties

This has to do with utilizing lands to raise animals and offer crops. Using this form of investment, investors can enjoy many of the benefits that come with the other standard form of real estate.

As an investor in agricultural properties, you can buy, sell, and lease agricultural properties. You can also become an agrarian business investor. For example, you can purchase a farm where you will produce crops and task the farmer with the responsibility of overseeing all the activities that go on in the farm. There are many agricultural properties you can capitalize on, which range from:

- **Farms**: These include portions of land used for agricultural needs like growing livestock, producing plants, and food.

- **Ranches**: This is just like a farm, but in contrast to a farm which is used for growing crops, ranches are only for raising livestock.

- **Orchards**: These include properties that contain various fruit trees which range from apples, to oranges, apricots, blueberries, and so on.

- **Timberland**: This agricultural property is filled with forest and is very suitable for timber. There are many opportunities available for you to invest in this kind of property which include exchange-traded funds (ETFs), or real estate investment trusts (REITs) which consist of products that have to do with timber.

Residential Properties

These are properties used for residential purposes. Some of these range from:

- **Single-family Homes**: Examples of homes in this category include detached or attached homes. As a real estate investor, this is the most popular option for investing in residential property at your disposal.

- **Apartment Buildings**: Another great form of residential property which is referred to as a multifamily unit. These properties can accommodate a lot of individuals in crowded areas. These buildings are prevalent in urban and suburban regions. However, it is not so common to locate any building that looks like an apartment building in any rural area. What's more, there may be security, clubhouses, swimming pools, and parking, among other amenities. If you want the least amount of risk, ease in management, and competition, this is the way to go. However, you will need a higher amount of capital to invest in this type of property in comparison to other real estate properties.

- **Condominium**: These also go by the name condos, and they share a lot of similarities with apartment buildings. But the major difference is in its ownership. Condos have private ownership, while apartment buildings are owned by businesses or solitary owners. Condos have homeowners associations (HOA) tasked with the responsibility of handling the maintenance of the building. What's more, you can find all of the features that come with apartments in condos like swimming pools, elevators, and tennis courts, among other things.

- **Factory-Built Homes**: These also go by the name manufactured homes. These are constructed from scratch in the factory, transferred to the intended location, and set up. The U.S Department of Housing and Urban Development has the task of administering and managing properties such as these. As a result of how they are developed, these properties are more budget-friendly and more enticing to buyers. This is because of the modern concepts incorporated into these kinds of structures.

- **Conversion Properties**: These also go by the name converted-use properties. These structures are those that have been converted to be utilized as residential properties. These structures could be ones that served other purposes before they were renovated into residential structures.

- **Cooperative**: These real properties are unique from other forms of real estate. By investing in a property such as this, you will be included in a corporation that owns the property. There will be other investors in this corporation like you, and all of you will be called shareholders. All shareholders are qualified to live in a housing unit depending on what is written in the shareholder agreement.

- **Planned Unit Developments (PUDs)**: These are building developments which may come with a complete residence. It can be utilized for industrial parks, commercial centers, and recreation parks. If investors can get the appropriate permits, they can take advantage of the space in developments by reducing the sizes of lots and street locations.

Commercial Properties

These are properties that function for business activities like hotels, stores, shopping centers, and so on. Some of the major types of commercial properties include:

- **Business Property**: This includes properties that are owned and managed by organizations. These properties could be where a business is set up or carries out its operations.

- **Shopping Centers**: These include properties that involve retail. Many investors search for these forms of properties to invest their resources in.

- **Office Space**: These include properties that have spaces where business activities take place.

- **Hotels**: These are common investment properties for many investors. Most investors invest in these properties in a bid to expand their real estate portfolio.

Industrial Properties

These are properties used for industrial purposes. Many investors do not like the idea of investing in these kinds of property. Nonetheless, if you can invest in the right industrial properties, the possibilities are endless. Some of the primary forms of industrial properties are:

- **Warehouses**: These buildings function for storing goods and resources. But warehouses go beyond just storing goods for lengthy periods. Rather, warehouses usually have a lot of activity and are utilized in making sure goods and products continue to get to customers that need them. This can offer investors with tons of opportunities if they can invest in the right one.

- **Factories**: These buildings accommodate the equipment and machinery used for producing goods. Many investors fail to see the possibilities behind these structures, but they offer a range of potentials.

Other property options include:

Mixed-Use

These include properties that can be used for more than one purpose. For instance, a building that functions as both a commercial and residential property.

Special Purpose Property

These are properties with public ownership like parks, government buildings, and so on.

The above are some of the major options you have to choose from. But knowing the kind of property you want is just one aspect of real estate success. You still need to know who to purchase these properties from for the best result. We will break this down in the next chapter.

Chapter 3: Individuals You Should Buy Properties From

In real estate, knowing who to purchase a property from is exceptionally crucial. This is because buying a property from the wrong person can put you in a financial mess. However, if you purchase from the right source, it could bring you substantial ROI down the road.

In this chapter, we will cover some of the key places you can buy real estate properties. They include:

- Buying from owners with equity
- Purchasing from owners without equity
- Buying foreclosed homes at auction
- Buying foreclosures owned by a bank
- Purchasing from absentee owners with equity

Buying from Owners with Equity

Life never goes as smoothly as we want, and this is the case with many homeowners. There are situations which may arise which will result in a homeowner requiring a means to find urgent cash. Many of these issues are usually not planned for and are beyond the control of these homeowners, some of which range from divorce, health issues, death, financial problems, and a change in environment. When these occur, homeowners may need to sell their property at a price much lower than the market value of the property.

Yet, before you purchase properties from owners with equity, especially those dealing with financial problems, there are a few things to note. First, the mortgage they owe may be way above the cost of the property. This means they won't be able to dispose of the property to you at a fair price and still pay off their mortgage. But if you go with those who owe a little part of their property's cost as a mortgage, you can get a good deal. Homeowners in this category are those who don't have much debt, which means their property has equity. This urges them to sell as fast as they can to raise funds to meet up with their needs and offset their mortgage simultaneously. Purchasing properties from individuals in this category is a better option, as they give you the chance to negotiate a better deal.

Purchasing from Owners without Equity

Owners without equity are those who have mortgage debt which is more than what their property costs and have been unable to meet up with repayment. In this situation, the homeowners have no other choice than to start a short sale process. The process begins with the homeowner giving approval to a lender or property to sell their property at a price lower than what is owed to the lender.

The process of short sale is appealing to banks because it is not time-consuming and is very budget-friendly. For most banks, this option is better than going through a foreclosure, because foreclosure requires investment in terms of time and finance. Besides, when a short sale is over, everybody is a winner, which is unlike the foreclosure process, which may not bring in as much as a short sale would.

Buying Foreclosed Homes at Auctions

If you are an investor with many years of experience under your belt, then this is a great place to buy from. If you are new to real estate investment, this may not be an ideal option for you because of the intricacies involved. Experienced investors can determine if it is worth purchasing a property and will likely have access to lots of amazing deals. In contrast, new investors may be unable to understand all of the requirements, which may result in them purchasing the wrong property, leading them to financial loss.

Also, even though buying this kind of property can provide you with long term benefits, there is also a major drawback involved. The instant you become the owner of a foreclosed property, you also take up ownership of all the claims, debts, and liens associated with the property. Depending on the kind of property, this can take a deep dive into your earnings.

Buying Foreclosures Owned by a Bank

Bank-owned foreclosures are also recognized as REO. They are properties that have passed through the process of foreclosure but were unable to get the interest of a buyer during the auction. When this happens, the bank makes efforts to dispose of the property via real estate. To do this, the bank gets the help of a real estate agent to aid in listing the product to dispose of it fast. Then, the agent lists the structure on an MLS (multiple listing service), and when anyone is interested in the property, they indicate this by sending offers to the agent. This is similar to the way it works when buyers are interested in other forms of properties.

Though, in contrast to the typical method of buying properties, an asset manager is responsible for going through the offers and overseeing the sales process. The asset manager has the authority to either reject or accept an offer during the sales process. But he or she does not have the final approval, as there are top bank officials charged with the responsibility of giving the final consent. The instant the offer gets approval, a contract will be signed, and the structure will be closed. The closing process requires at least three weeks or more for it to be finalized.

Purchasing from Absentee Owners with Equity

Many homeowners do not become one by choice. For some, it was an inheritance which they were unable to sell, while some relocated but were unable to dispose of the property. Due to this, they had to put it up for rent as a means of generating income instead of holding on to the property. If you can find these individuals, buying from them is a great option.

Which is the Best One for You?

There is certainly an option which is more suitable for you than others. To determine the best choice for you, there are a few things you need to consider which include the following.

Your Time Frame

Before you make a choice, you need to determine how long you want the project to last. Is it one you need to complete in a hurry, or one you are okay taking as much time as needed with? If the time duration is not vital for you, it's best to go with a short sale or REO. If time is of the essence, an auctioned property should do just fine. Regardless of what your option is, your timeframe will be a great determinant of the choice you decide to go with.

Your Nature

What kind of individual are you? Are you fine with communication with individuals you don't know? Do you have a lot of empathy? If this is the case, then you may be able to purchase from homeowners with equity. If this is not the case, then you may be better suited for other choices that don't directly have to do with homeowners. You need to determine the kind of personality you have and how it can impact your business before you choose a type of seller.

Your Location

Your residence is also of vital importance. Do you reside in a location where there are lots of homeowners with equity? If yes, look for homeowners who have issues offsetting mortgages. When searching for who to buy from, look into the condition of the real estate market, and the area you reside, as all of these can help you choose the best seller for you.

When you have covered the ideal seller to choose and who to purchase from, the next step is to find a great real estate investment deal. The chapter below will cover this in detail.

Chapter 4: Locating The Best Real Estate Investment Deals

To be a successful real estate investor, you need to know how to find the best deals available. If you can always point out where to find profitable investment opportunities, you will always set yourself for high ROI each time. Knowing this, below are a few of the top options for finding deals.

Check the Local Newspaper

Newspapers are not as popular as they once were. This does not mean they are not still a great place to search. If you are looking to purchase For Sale by Owner (FSBO) properties, then the classifieds section in your local newspaper is a great place to search.

The only drawback of looking for deals using the newspaper is that searching through listings can be very difficult. Unlike other online methods, there is no way to sort out listings by any specific category, and you need to search one at a time manually. If you do have enough energy and time to go through this time-consuming process, then this is an option that you may find suitable.

Checkout Pocket Listings

Pocket listings consist of deals that have not been listed by agents and brokers on the market. This is more common in commercial and residential deals which are not marketable. Brokers may decide not to openly market a deal because they don't want to get the existing management or tenants scared. If the tenants see a home they presently reside in being marketed, they may feel a rent increase is on the way, which may result in many of them mobbing to other properties. The implication of this will be a reduction in the Net Operating Income of the property, which makes it a less marketable one. If you can link yourself with brokers who have connections, you can build a relationship with them and urge them to place you on their buyer's list.

Word of Mouth

To date, this remains one of the best methods of marketing and selling things. There are still products which are sold using this method, and it is one that is here to stay. This means you can use this method to locate great deals. If you tell every one of your connections you are looking for a property to buy, you may get some information regarding properties that have not been listed yet. There may be someone who knows the home of a friend about to be sold but has not yet been listed on the market. With this, you get yourself a property with less competition at the best prices. You can use this strategy with people you know, those in the same line of business as you, or at any real estate event or club you attend.

Direct Mail

This means of finding deals is not one that everyone seems to agree with. To use this method, you buy a mailing list which includes names and contact information of homeowners who may likely sell. Then you reach out to these owners via written letters, which you then send through the mail with the hopes that one of them will get back to you. Many people find this intrusive, which is why it is not a commonly accepted method.

What's more, it has a meager response rate. But those who use this method work with the idea that of all the homeowners who get their mail, they will get a response from one and a closed deal. If time is not a factor for you, then this is an excellent option to try out.

Drive Around Neighborhoods

If you want to find residential as well as commercial properties, taking a drive around can be a good option. Choose the area of your choice, take a drive around it, and determine the properties that seem like they are under duress. The reason for this is simple; homeowners of distressed properties have a higher tendency to sell in comparison to others.

Determining a distressed property is not difficult. Watch out for abandoned cars, overgrown shrubs, and property damage that seem to have been ignored for a long time. If you can spot a property with signs such as this, you can approach the homeowner, and perhaps find yourself a great deal.

Use Cold Calls

This is similar to contacting the potential seller via mail. But instead of using mail, here you get a list and call them instead. There is a range of online services willing to offer you this information. You can find the phone number of a person using an address through a concept called skip-tracing.

Try Property Management Corporations

Some organizations manage properties all around the country. You are likely to find one close to you. These corporations have a broad reach in the city they are located in. What's more, they have knowledge of all the streets, areas, and leading realtors in a specific area. This means once there is a home available for sale, these corporations will be one of the first to find out. If you can manage to align yourself with an organization such as this, there is a huge possibility of finding a homeowner who has a great deal for you.

Also, these corporations manage every kind of property, including those that seem to be under distress and deteriorating.

If you have a little capital for investment into developing such properties, these organizations may be willing to reach out to the property owners on your behalf.

Eviction Courts

This option is not one which is quite popular. Many people may currently be dealing with an eviction they are already tired of and are in search of a means to sell their properties.

If you can make yourself available to them during their time of need, they may be willing to sell the property so they don't have to deal with the trouble of frustrating tenants.

Connect with a Title Company

These are organizations that know a great deal about the market, and if you can develop a relationship with an organization like this, they can assist you in finding a vast number of transactions you can benefit from in the long run.

They have information on all the leaders in your neighborhood who want to sell off their property. These kinds of companies are ideal if you want to get real estate deals that are not on the market. This is also beneficial to both parties, as you can provide them with more business once the deal has been finalized and closed.

Try Apartment or Landlord Association Meetings

As a real estate investor, having a great network can continuously provide you with numerous benefits. One of these is to help you find fantastic market listings. One of the ways you can do this is through a landlord or apartment meeting. In these kinds of meetings, you will have direct interaction with homeowners and may be able to get information on one who is willing to sell.

Landlords who are conversant with how the market works may not be willing to let go of their properties at a reduced price. Nevertheless, they can offer you owner financing, which can be beneficial to you both. In essence, even if you are unable to buy the property at low market value, you may likely get excellent owner financing terms which make certain that the landlord does not pay excess capital gains.

Real Estate Investing Meetings

These are meetings filled with real estate investors. They also have to do with marketing, as you will be communicating with other investors like yourself. If you build good relationships, you may run into an investor who knows about a deal he or she has no finances to see through, or no interest whatsoever. This investor can offer you details of the deal, or you can both collaborate as partners. No matter the option you choose to go with, the result will be beneficial to you.

Tax Delinquencies

If a homeowner can't meet up with tax payments any longer, many of them will want to dispose of their property before it goes to the city. This information is public and can be accessed by anyone who wants it. Also, numerous services can aid you in developing lists. All that will be left for you after that is to make cold calls, send direct mail, or drive around the property. You can find great deals with this option.

Multiple Listing Service (MLS)

The MLS is a good place for finding amazing deals, even though many investors seem to think otherwise. What's more, you can create a relationship with a free broker and ask them to recommend amazing property managers to you, while you do the same. This way, even if you don't get deals, you can keep up communication and something might come up in the future.

Vendors

Vendors work on properties during renovation, and sometimes they sell materials for building. In most instances, they will know top property owners and the best neighborhoods in a city. These people can inform you about properties that are under distress, or whose owners want to sell.

Social Media

The popularity of social media cannot be understated, and many sellers in varying sectors are starting to take advantage of what it offers. It is a great way to connect with a huge audience at once. Many real estate investors who did not notice how helpful social media platforms could be have now learned how easy finding good deals can be on these various platforms. If you know where to look, this is undoubtedly a great place to find leads.

Real Estate Attorneys

When a homeowner wants to sell off his or her property, they reach out to a real estate attorney. This is the case notwithstanding their motivation for selling the property. There are numerous reasons why people sell which range from divorce, eviction, foreclosure, and so on.

In most instances, real estate attorneys are some of the first individuals to find out about properties that are up for sale. If you can develop great relationships with attorneys in your neighborhood, they can provide you with access to that deal that may bring you colossal ROI.

Finding a great deal may need commitment and time. Yet, the benefits you stand to gain are enormous. The above are some of the best options at your disposal to help you find that deal you desire.

Ensuring You Profit after Your Investment

To make a good ROI from what you buy, you will need to purchase the property at a price that brings you good returns after selling. This means you have to be smart when purchasing property, and an efficient way of doing this is to run the numbers.

If you pay too much for a property, you won't make a good ROI no matter how much you develop the property or the level of work you put in. You can leverage the information you learn on the present market to help you determine if the investment you are making is a profitable one.

At this point, you should be fully conversant with the option(s) you want to go with. But, even if you find the right option now, you may not be able to afford your desired property. This is where putting your finance in place becomes vital, and we will cover this next.

Chapter 5: Getting Real Estate Investment Finance

Similar to other forms of investment, finance is a vital aspect of real estate. However, for a lot of real estate investors, knowing the best sources of funding is a huge hindrance. This is why it is essential to learn where to get the finances for your real estate investment, as this can have a lot of impact on if your venture is a success or not.

In this chapter, we will be delving into all of your finance options as an investor in real estate. But before we go any further, let's have a look at some of the things you have to understand before you get a real estate loan.

Real Estate Loans: Important Things to Understand

For investors who want to take advantage of investments, loans are usually the first options for finance. The reason for this is that real estate investment requires a substantial amount of cash. This can be difficult for many investors to fund by themselves without access to loans. Nonetheless, before you go in search of a loan for your investment, there are a few things you need to note, especially if you want a rehab loan. Home rehab loans are short term loans provided by individuals or private firms to people who have an interest in purchasing properties and renovating them before they dispose of it for profit. The guidelines we will be discussing below will aid you in getting these loans from issuers.

If you have plans to borrow cash from a lender, you will need to provide the issuing individual or firm with elaborate information on all of the properties you want to invest in. Having a business plan in place at this point will make this less complicated. With a business plan, the process is smooth and fast. A business plan does not have to be complicated; nonetheless, it is essential for it to include the following:

- Where the property is situated or address
- A look into the neighborhood or area
- Comps
- A plan B in the event the primary plan does not go accordingly
- Scope of work
- Expert evaluation of the home you want to purchase by an appraiser

If your business plan deals with all of these areas in detail, there will be a higher possibility of your proposal being taken more seriously.

Get a Correct Estimate of the Amount You Will Need for Renovating the Property

Before you take the step to apply for a loan, you need to have a precise estimate of the amount you will require for renovation. This is necessary because many investors get stranded mid-way into a project because they did not borrow enough funds. If you don't want to fall into this trap, you need to have a scope of work in place. Scope of work has to do with comprehensive information about all the repairs you plan on carrying out on a property, the cost, and the timeline. You will have to get the help of a professional appraiser and a licensed contractor to put the scope of work in place. These experts can offer you an estimated timeline, and cost of renovations, after doing extensive research using a comparable project.

Build Your Network

When it has to do with real estate, the connections you have to play a huge role. To get the best out of this, you can become a member of real estate clubs and associations close to you. This will get you closer to other investors, which can push you one step closer to success. If you want to break ground in real estate, you must have a robust network, because investors and lenders have more tendency to collaborate with well-known investors. Besides, there are investors in real estate who loan funds from lenders to invest in the projects being carried out by other investors.

Best Sources of Financing

There is a range of sources to get finance as a real estate investor. Here, we will be looking into some of the major sources you can tap from.

Get Loans from Family or Friends

When you want to access finance for your real estate investment, the first and most comfortable place to look is your immediate family and friends. These could range from your siblings, close friends, or friends of friends. You will be surprised as to how many of these people will be willing to invest in your venture. Getting finance from your family and friends is one of the best places to start. This is because they will probably request a lower rate of interest because of the personal relationship between you two.

Nonetheless, when getting loans from people close to you, it is best to follow a few protocols. This will ensure you don't fall into issues down the road. The first step you will need to take is to obtain an agreement in writing which clearly states the rate of interest and length of repayment. When you have a written agreement in place, it will safeguard the lender as well as yourself if an issue crops up. When it has to do with money, even our closest friends can quickly become enemies in the event of a misunderstanding. If you cherish the relationship you both share, there should be no question about this. Next, make sure you are in compliance with all the securities and IRS laws that have to do with family investments.

There are an array of factors that will determine the loan terms, and these factors vary depending on the loan amount, your relevant geographic market, and the requirements of the property. Also important is the readiness of the borrower to delve into risk and the level of experience you have. In most instances, the borrower does not have to pay anything when the building is being worked on; however, he or she will need to pay the overall amount, and the interest garnered after disposing of the property. In a situation where the borrower reneges on the agreement put in place, the house will act as a form of collateral.

Tap into Your 401(k)

This is another excellent way to get finance for your investment project. Loan some funds or borrow from your 401(k) account. If you are close to retirement, this may not be the right option for you. It is excellent for those who are still very young and not yet close to retirement. The repercussions can be terrible if you exhaust all of the funds in your 401(k) account only to be left with nothing after retirement.

If you choose to go with this option, you have the chance to get a loan of around 50% of the balance in your account, or $50,000, depending on which is less. If you are an entrepreneur and have a 401(k) account, you can also access a $50,000 loan. The great thing about taking loans from your 401(k) is that the principal you are paying goes back to you. This makes it a win-win option of finance. As an alternative, it is possible to obtain a loan by tapping into your life insurance policy to finance your real estate project.

Use Personal Loans

A personal loan offers you another flexible method of getting real estate investment finance. This loan is similar to a typical business loan which allows you to use the loan for any kind of business, and real estate investment is no exception. To be eligible to access a personal loan, it is essential for you to have an excellent credit score above 650.

What's more, you get a low rate of interest, and some offer you 5% which you can pay every month, spread around a three to seven year period. Another critical aspect of a personal loan you need to consider is that the loan is not usually large. There is a $50,000 cap which may be inadequate if you are financing a large project. This means it may be essential to use it alongside other methods of financing to complete a project.

Find Yourself a Financing Partner

For many real estate investors, one major problem they deal with is that they have the knowledge and skills to spot a profitable investment property and make it work, but they do not have the finances to see it through. If you ever fall into a situation like this, the experience can be very frustrating. To get around this, you have the option of collaborating with a financing partner who has the required finances and is willing to assist you.

You and your financing partner can split the duties below:

- Look for profitable opportunities for investment
- Provide finance for the investment
- Oversee the project

Ultimately, the profit is shared between all of the contributors based on what they did to ensure the project was successful. In most instances, one person is tasked with looking for suitable areas to invest, while the other finances the project. It is up to you to use one partner to finance every project you come across or use multiple partners. The partner tasked with providing financing of the project is provided with their share depending on their negotiation power. If they provide finance by themselves without assistance from other partners, they get around 30% - 50% of the overall profit. But, in the event of a loss, it will be shared among the collaborating partners as well, even though they hardly occur.

For example, if your partner provides financing for a rehab investment project worth $200,000, and you did not add a dime, if you sell the home at a loss of say $150,000, you and your partner will have to share the loss using the sharing formula put in place. This makes it vital to have an agreement in place in instances when plans don't go how you projected.

A Business Line of Credit

If you go with the option of a business line of credit, you will get the flexibility that typical loans do not provide. This is what makes it a common choice for investors in real estate. What's more, you only need to pay interest on the amount of cash you loan. The concept behind this is similar to using credit cards; you take the money you require and pay it back at your convenience.

If you are investing in home rehabbing and are uncertain of how long the process will take, then this is your best bet. Depending on your experience, the income of your business, and your portfolio, a business line of credit can be as much as seven figures.

There are a set of banks that provide business lines of credits to investors, some of which include Bank of America (BOA), and WellsFargo, among many others. These loans come with a very minimal rate of interest. However, you need an excellent credit score, a consistent source of income, and a decent amount of cash in your account to be eligible for this loan.

Home Equity Loan (HEL)

If you are a homeowner, an excellent way to get finance is to get a home equity loan. This loan is also called Home Equity Line of Credit (HELOC). With HEL, you can get funding for your real estate investment. This offers more benefits than typical loans because the interest you pay depends on the amount you spend. You can get loans using HELOC depending on the amount you require, and you can get it at any point you need it. This is in contrast to a loan, which is a lump sum of cash you borrow at a go.

The market value of your property and your mortgage balance is the equity. However, to be eligible for a HELOC, you require home equity of at least 20%. But if the amount of cash you want to borrow is massive, you may need over the average 20% equity alongside reasonable monthly earnings, and fair credit which is adequate to pay off your HEL and mortgage.

Many banks loan you around 85% of the value of your property and deduct it from your remaining loan balance. For instance, if you have an equity of 20%, and a property worth $300,000, you will owe a mortgage of $240,000. This means you are eligible for as much as $50,000 HELOC or HEL. If this will be inadequate for you to finish your project, its best to search for an alternative means of financing to merge with this.

Real Estate Crowdfunding

In the past, only those who were extremely wealthy could invest in real estate. However, all of this changed after the JOBS Act of 2012 was passed. After this, investors took the chance to partake in crowdfunding to ensure they were able to invest at a reduced cost. A good amount of investors use this method by keeping an eye out for projects available on crowdfunding platforms. Then, they become a partner by contributing to projects that pique their interests. Contributions can be even as little as $1,000. The instant the project is over, contributors are given their share from any of the profit obtained.

But, you need to understand that real estate crowdfunding comes with some possible dangers. As an investor, there is nothing you can do about the outcome of the investment. Furthermore, the waiting period for ROI may not be as fast as you projected, and if things do not go as planned, only investors are responsible for the losses.

Seller Financing

Seller financing, which is also categorized as owner financing, is an instance where a property owner finances a property sale. This is in contrast to the conventional means of loans where the buyer obtains a bank mortgage. When sellers are enthusiastic about disposing of their properties fast, this is the option they typically turn to. This form of financing offers benefits to both individuals involved. With this, a seller can dispose of his or her property quickly and attain high ROI. On the other hand, buyers enjoy better loan conditions and terms, more flexible downpayment requirement, and an adjustable rate. It is an excellent alternative to the conventional means of selling a property in a credit market, which is very harsh.

Here, the seller acts as the lender during the process. Nonetheless, instead of offering the buyer cash, the homeowner provides the buyer credit to match the property's selling price after both of the individuals involved sign a promissory note which consists of all the loan terms and conditions. Furthermore, both parties head to the public records office to record a deed of mortgage or trust. In terms of repayment, the buyer pays back alongside interest over time.

The loan is not one which lasts for a long time. Instead, it is short term. For example, the loan can be amortized over 20 years, but with a balloon payment of 3 years. In essence, in a few years, the value of the property should have gone up, or the buyer's financial situation should have gotten better to the level that the two parties can refinance with a typical lender. To ensure there is no confusion along the line, similar to other sources of finance, it is best to get a written agreement. Better still, if you have the means, you can get the services of a licensed real estate attorney to help with putting the loan papers together.

Small Business Association Loans (SBA)

Small Business Association loans are loans offered by the SBA with an assurance to pay banks that give loans to owners of new business. This assurance serves as a form of collateral for the banks, and due to this, they offer these loans even with the possible risk.

The ability to access loans has a lot to do with your situation as an investor; however, it is possible to loan as much as $2 million. Besides, the repayment plan for SBA loans is quite flexible and can be spread out through many years. It offers you the option of providing reduced downpayment and also safeguards you from huge fees. With all of these, your business can flourish, and you can easily maintain cash flow.

However, SBA loans do not apply to an investment in real estate. Nonetheless, if you want to start a real estate business, then it can work. SBA only offer loans to owners of real estate businesses like brokers or property managers. The loan comes with a high rate of interest, alongside possibly lengthy application processes and other conditions. Some of these conditions range from having incredible profit on tax returns, and a remarkable credit score among others.

Hard Money Loans

This is another common form of getting financing for a real estate investment project. This is dependent on assets through which a lender gets the cash secured using real property. Private investors issue these loans, and they are great options for borrowers who are unable to get loans from standard lenders but need the loans fast. When it comes to hard money lending, the capacity of the borrower to pay back the loan is not essential because the lenders have more interest in the worth of the collateral.

The fact that lenders of hard money loans do not have as much interest in the borrower's financial position means their loan requirements are not as harsh as standard lenders; however, the attached interest rates are more than usual. The rate of interest is dependent on the lender, nevertheless it can be as much as 20%. Typically, hard money loans can last for as long as one year or two, and can sometimes be as long as five years. These loans are offered only to sort our property renovations, but the instant you sell the property, the loan ends. You need to pay interest each month for hard money loans, alongside a balloon payment when the loan term ends.

Before you decide to go with the option of a hard money loan, it is essential that you do some research and be sure of what you are getting into. Although the high rates of interests may be daunting, it remains an excellent means of getting the funds you need fast.

Collaborate with a Mortgage Broker

An excellent option for getting finance is to work with a mortgage broker. This option is ideal if you don't want to deal with the hassle of finding the right lender. A mortgage broker can aid in your loan application by applying for loans from numerous lenders. He or she also helps you compare the various rates for the best option. If you work alongside a mortgage broker to finance your real estate investment, there are a range of benefits you stand to gain:

- They are linked with a variety of lenders which you may not even know existed.

- A mortgage lender can find you lenders with the best terms for repayment and make sure you don't collect loans from hidden clauses in the contract.

- Some lenders won't work with you if you are not a mortgage lender. Furthermore, these lenders tend to listen to mortgage lenders to determine the real estate investor to work alongside.

Going with the mortgage lender also means you have to understand a few things which may not be in your favor:

- The mortgage broker may be after his or her interest, which may not be in your favor. Mortgage brokers make their money from commission, and their goal may be to get the highest possible. However, your goal will be to obtain the best rate of interest and fees, and your desires may not align.

- Some lenders choose not to work alongside mortgage brokers because they feel these mortgages from brokers may likely default payments in contrast to direct lending.

- You may not be able to get access to lenders who would have offered you better than what you would get from the mortgage broker. This would have been different if you did it by yourself.

Choosing the Best Option

Getting financing for your real estate investment does not have to be complicated. It is even easier if you know where to search. When choosing the best option, do not forget that it has a lot to do with your present state of finance, the type of property you want to buy, and the objectives you have as an investor in real estate.

Having understood the sources of finance available to you, it does not mean your work is done. Real estate investment is not a one-person task, mainly if you aim to expand your business. However, a team of professionals can help you make this process easier. This makes it vital to put the appropriate team together, which is what we will be discussing in the chapter to follow.

Chapter 6: Putting Your Real Estate Team Together

Even the most straightforward real estate investment deals can be entirely consuming and taxing for one person to handle effectively. There are many things to consider, which is undoubtedly too much for a single individual. Furthermore, if you aim to grow and carry out more extensive projects, you will need help. This is where selecting the appropriate team comes into play. With the right team behind you, achieving the objectives you have put in place becomes seamless.

Below, we will be delving into a few tips to help you pick your team members, and a few important details to note. First, a look at what your real estate investment team helps you with.

How Does a Real Estate Investment Team Help You?

Real estate investment teams consist of experts that you collaborate with before and after you invest in real estate projects. These team members can aid you in doing research on a property, providing you with financing, and locating good deals. This will ensure you can focus on other more critical aspects of your project. However, you need to pick only relevant and reliable professionals for your team, as the wrong team members can make your project go longer than it should while costing you finances. That being said, who are the professionals you need to include in your team?

Professionals to Include in Your Team

To get the best ROI your investment can offer, it is ideal that you get a dependable team willing to support you in areas you require. Your team has to be experienced, skilled, and motivated enough to help you get the best deals on the market, and finance your investment.

Vital professionals to be included in your team are:

Real Estate Agents

These are some of the first professionals that should be included in your team. They can help ensure your business gets to the height it should be at due to how experienced they are in the real estate sector. These experts know the best places to locate properties and find great deals. They also have expertise in helping you reach prospective buyers, making sure you get top deals, and helping sell your property fast.

What should you look for when choosing a real estate agent?

When choosing a real estate agent for your team, you want a person who would desire the best interest for you and your business. This is why you need to go with the best realtor you can find. Below are some tips that can aid you in choosing the right agent:

- **Proper license**: Look for an agent licensed to practice in the state they are in. This is something you can easily find out by heading to the real estate commission site for the state you are in. By going with one who is appropriately licensed, you can be sure there are no potential lawsuits on your hands. This is because, with the connections they have established during their career, they can learn some vital information which they can use to the advantage of your business.

- **Knowledge of the market**: Go with an agent who thoroughly understands the real estate market in your region. With an experienced agent by your side, you can get a professional perspective of a potential market. Besides, they can help you find great real estate deals which you can make a profit from.

- **A clear line of communication**: When it comes to real estate investment, time is critical. For this reason, you need to get an agent with a clear line of communication. Ensure you choose an agent who is available and okay with your preferred means of communication. Projects can arise at any moment, and you want a real estate agent you can reach fast without any hassle.

- **Go with your gut**: Ultimately, you have to go with someone you are comfortable working alongside. Including a professional real estate agent in your team means you plan to work with them for the long term. This makes it vital to choose an agent your gut goes with, and who understands your needs.

Contractors

A contractor is a team member you can't do without. The reason is that they have the responsibility of carrying out estimates on your project cost. If your properties require repairs or serious renovation, a great contractor can point it out and work on them as well. Finding the appropriate contractors can be a little tricky, so you need to make sure that you get one which is reliable and budget-friendly. To get the right fit, its best to do elaborate research on all of the contractors close to you offering the best price.

Choosing a Contractor

The following tips can help you choose the right contractor to include in your real estate team. They include:

- **Find out if they have comprehensive insurance and license**: Before you select a general contractor, make sure that their license is up to date. Also, find out if they have insurance. You want a contractor who you will be working with in the long term, and if you go with one who has no license or insurance, you may be stuck with expenses you did not bargain for down the line. Be sure that any contractor you choose is bonded to you in the event they fail to pay for permits, finish up a project, cause damage on the site, among many other things. Also, going with a contractor who has insurance in place will ensure you are protected if something goes wrong during your project.

- **Search your neighborhood**: It is always a good idea to go with a contractor you can easily access. Find one who you can easily access when you need to. If you are going to include a contractor on your team, it should be one within driving distance. Contact local businesses and find out about how involved the contractor is in the communities around them. If a contractor cares about the community they are based in, there is a high possibility that they will channel the same level of care to any project you provide.

- **Check out their reviews**: Many good contractors have the right online presence to prove it. However, you need to go beyond looking into their online presence by going through their online reviews. With the reviews, you can tell if a contractor has had a satisfactory history or is shoddy at his job. There will be customers who will be glad to share their experiences with contractors to help you make the right choice.

- **Determine their level of experience**: Before you include a contractor on your team, be certain they are experienced in the kind of job you need them for. Some contractors have handled projects of various sizes and have a lot of experience under their belt. By going with a contractor who has vast experience, you can be certain he or she will be able to handle any project you throw their way. Also, find out if they have been in a team beforehand. If they have, the better it is for you, as their experience can be beneficial to you as well.

Appraisers and Inspectors

Both of these experts should not be overlooked, as they can help you determine a property's market cost, cost of repair, and the profit you can get from the project. These professionals can also aid you in determining the amount a property can generate in a specific neighborhood if you decide to rent it out. They are individuals with vital knowledge of properties in your area and can help you find out if the contractor is providing you with the appropriate cost estimate. It is easy to locate these individuals with the assistance of other investors close to you.

When choosing an inspector, go with someone who is licensed. Go through their records in the state licensing agency to find out if there have been any complaints on their record. Inspectors with the proper licenses do not come cheap; however, the price you pay is worth it. Your inspector has the responsibility of finding any downside to a property that you would not have spotted on your own. Go through the website of the inspector, alongside their Yelp and Google reviews. This will help you determine the kind of inspectors you are dealing with. You can also run a search for your inspector on Facebook and Google, where individuals have a higher tendency to leave reviews of the work done.

Finally, you want to have knowledge of the areas your inspector will inspect, as well as what areas they are more knowledgeable in. This way, even if you are not going to be on the premises, you will be sure that your inspector will do an expert and thorough job.

Wholesalers

Similar to real estate agents, wholesalers can aid you in locating the best deals. They can also offer you the data you need on the top locations to invest. Wholesalers purchase properties on a contract, which they then transfer to you and other investors in real estate as a way to make a profit. This makes it necessary to network with other wholesalers around you to enable you to access deals anytime they are available. With this, you can save money and time. You will also find deals much quicker. The great part of working with a wholesaler is that you don't need to bother about any extensive research as the wholesaler takes up responsibility for this.

Lenders

As you must understand by now, real estate investments, particularly huge ones, require large amounts of cash. Furthermore, the more money you put in, the more you can profit. In essence, getting finance from lenders will help you earn more money since there is ready cash. A lender with the proper experience can provide you with funding, which can come in loans that can spread through a period of 30 years (single asset) or 10 years (fixed portfolio).

If you can access these kinds of loans, you will have the capacity to invest in a higher number of projects, or the ability to refinance the ones you already have.

Bookkeepers

Similar to any business, keeping records in your real estate investment project is essential. A bookkeeper can help you out in this area by keeping tabs on expenses, income, debits, and your credits. Furthermore, they can also help you prepare your finances for tax payment. All of these are crucial areas for ensuring your business runs smoothly.

CPA (Certified Public Accountant)

A CPA can offer you the best strategy for saving on tax payments. They can also help with the preparation of your personal and business tax returns. If you have a CPA in your team, it can be beneficial to ensuring your project is a success.

Lawyers

Lawyers are also quite vital. They can help in putting together all of the legal documents in your project. This will ensure there are no loopholes or hidden lines in your contract. Having a lawyer with experience in the real estate sector is not to be overlooked.

Property Managers

Property managers can help with the management of your properties, which makes their presence necessary. They can offer you immense benefits, particularly if you have a considerable number of investment projects on your hands. They can aid in solving problems with tenants, and help you deal with complex or time-consuming tasks so you can focus on other things. You must do a comprehensive search so you get the best property manager for your project.

General Handyman

The importance of having a general handyman cannot be over-emphasized. If you can, it is best to have two or more handymen on your list of contacts. You want someone always available and willing to handle the more minor jobs that can't be done by a contractor. If you have a rental property, you can have your tenants contact your handyman directly whenever an issue crops up. This way, you free yourself from the extra stress.

If you can develop a great relationship with handymen and continuously give them jobs, with time, they will be readily available to work on your project. Handymen will be glad to deal with problems that can hamper the progress of your project, even though they are minor ones. The presence of these experts will save you a lot of stress in the long run.

Pest Control Company

In real estate, there is a high chance that you will have to face the hassle of pests at some point. Regardless of if it is rodents or bed bugs, having a professional pest company on your team that can handle any of these issues will be of great benefit to you in the long run.

Insurance Broker

Real estate insurance is complicated, particularly if you do not know what you are doing. This can even be much worse when your money is involved. A great insurance broker can help you obtain the right type of insurance for your type of investment properties.

The above are some of the best professionals you will need on your team. They will help you locate deal, close deals, finance them, and assist with regular maintenance. All of these are individuals you cannot overlook on your team. However, remember that you don't have to stick with any of these professionals until the end if things don't work out. You are allowed to let go of any professional who is not meeting your requirements and find another. It is your investment and should be treated as such without sentiments. If someone is not doing their job, feel free to let them go for another more reliable professional.

When Should You Build Your Team?

The right moment to get your team in place is Now! The moment you are ready to begin investing in real estate, you should make conscious efforts to put your team together. If you build your real estate investment team early, it can save you lots of stress, time, and money down the road. Besides, it will help you to develop relationships and ensure you are a success in the real estate investment venture. With the right real estate investment team, even your first project can be an immense success.

Where to Find Your Real Estate Investing Team

You can turn to various locations to locate your team members. An excellent place to begin is to attend real estate investment events and meetings close to you. You can also ask other individuals in the business of real estate, too. Better still, run a search online or become a member of real estate groups on Instagram, Facebook, and LinkedIn. Become a member of these groups, drop valuable comments, create great connections, and learn from more experienced investors where to locate other team members.

With your team in place, it is time to look into the real estate options you have available to you. The first and cheapest is real estate wholesaling, which is covered in the next chapter.

Chapter 7: Wholesaling Real Estate

Wholesaling is a real estate investment which does not require any downpayment. It is widespread and one of the simplest to understand. This is a form of real estate investment any individual can partake in due to how easy it is to understand. It has to do with placing a property under contract at a specific price, before disposing of the contract at an increased rate. This is a process that does not require that much effort in comparison to other forms of real estate investment.

In this type of investment, the only interest of the wholesaler is to fix the contract. The wholesaler does not have any plans to do any repairs on the project. For this deal to go seamlessly, the following are vital: the cost would be altered so that the transaction can be profitable to you, the wholesaler and the buyer. All that is required from you is to allocate the contract, which is a step which usually occurs for payment. You also have to keep in mind that the title company needs to be able to deal with double closings, dry closings, and contract assignment. Not every organization can handle this, so you need to make sure you go with a title company that can do all of these, as it is impossible to wholesale your property in the absence of this. In this chapter, we will be delving into real estate and the steps involved in wholesaling real estate. We will also be checking out the pros and cons, among many others — first, a look at some of the benefits of being a wholesaler.

Benefits of Being a Wholesale Investor

- To become a wholesale investor, you require minimal, or very little, of your own funds to start.

- It is swift to get returns from your investment, which may be different in other forms of investments like fix and flip.

- There is not much risk involved because the process is not time-consuming.

- All risks that have to do with the property have nothing to do with the wholesaler.

Drawbacks to Being a Wholesale Investor

- You need to do a lot of research

- It may be a little challenging to locate a buyer

- The rules and regulations do not stay the same for long.

- Your capacity to locate a buyer has an impact on your ability to find a deal.

Steps Involved in Wholesaling Real Estate

The following are the steps to follow if you want to be a real estate wholesaler.

Do Your Research

Similar to other forms of investment, the first thing you need to do is a comprehensive research of the entire process. Take the time to teach yourself about what the process entails, so you don't get sidelined by anything that crops up during the process. This is a step you need to cover before you even begin to look for a property. Network with other investors experienced in wholesaling real estate to get valuable insights. There are also tons of resources available on the Internet, which you can leverage to understand the process better. By getting yourself informed as regards what to expect, you will be better positioned to begin your wholesaling journey with a great start.

Develop a Buyer's List

This is a list which consists of prospective homebuyers, entrepreneurs, and investors. Building a buyer's list of prospects is not exactly easy, and you will leverage your skills in networking. If done correctly, the rewards will be worth the stress. A good buyer's list will make sure that you know where to find buyers for your deals. There are many ways to build your buyer's list, some of which include using your personal connections, bandit signs, and direct mail. Reach out to other professionals in your field to grow your network, and if you come across a possible lead, be certain to get down their contact details for future purposes.

Market to Sellers with the Desire to Sell

Once you have put a good buyer's list in place, the next step is to begin your search for homeowners looking to sell their property. Sellers are motivated to sell for several reasons ranging from an inherited property they have no idea what to use for, problems with repayment of a mortgage, divorce, and so on. Regardless of why they want to sell, getting a motivated seller is one of the best ways to get a property at a reasonable price. If you want to locate motivated sellers, you can try targeting lists of absentee owners, and those in foreclosure like we have discussed in earlier chapters. After creating a list of targets, strategize on the best way to market to them. Some of the best options you have at your disposal include cold calling and digital mail. These remain some of the best methods to reach motivated sellers even to date.

Get a Property Under Contract

After you have located a buyer who is willing to sell, the next step is to reach an agreement on the cost of the property, alongside other conditions. When negotiating the contract, you need to make sure you and the seller want the same thing. Be sure to add every bit of information in the agreement to prevent issues in the future. If you do not have the right level of legal know-how to see this through, it may be best to get the services of a legal expert for the best results.

Locate Your End Buyer

The instant the property has been placed under contract, you start your search to assign the contract to an interested buyer. If you are in luck, you will find one from the list you developed in earlier steps. Compile a list of comps to help you determine the price in your neighborhood. Also, you may need to estimate the likely cost of renovation on the property, and get the services of a title company to help with the title.

Next, begin to contact all of the prospective buyers you put down on your list. You need to remember that not every property will be appealing to the same category of buyers. If you have apartment buildings with minor repairs, they may be more appealing to buyers who want to put it up for rent. In contrast, a property that requires in-depth renovation may be more attractive to house flippers. Educate yourself on the various exit strategies available in real estate so you will have an idea on the kind of buyer that will be attracted to your deal.

Get the Contract Assigned

If you are in luck, finding a buyer won't take up so much of your time. The instant you have located one, you need to start developing and signing a contract agreement. Be sure to include the deposit amount agreed on, and the agreement fee when drawing up the final agreement. You want everything to be clearly stated in the event of a disagreement later on. Many people believe that the contract stage is complicated, but this is not the case. It is as easy as assigning the contract for a specified amount of cash. Doing this will ensure all parties are in agreement, and that you get the payment due to you.

Close the Deal

When the time comes for you to close the deal, be sure that your end buyer makes themselves available so they can sign the required documents. They need to come with the required forms and the money to buy the property. Also, make certain that they bring along your assignment fee. The instant the title company accepts payment from the buyer, they will draft out an amount covering your fee.

How to Know if Wholesaling a Property is Ideal for You

Wholesaling is best for individuals who do not have adequate finance but want to delve into the business of real estate. The reason for this is that wholesaling does not require any down-payment in comparison to other methods of real estate investing. It is also ideal for those who have the knack for locating properties that are under duress and are great at negotiations.

Before you go all-in into wholesaling real estate, it is vital to do extensive research on the sector beforehand. You will need to put in effort and time if you want to find sellers motivated to sell their properties. You will also need to locate other experienced real estate investors who can help in providing you with guidance. Lastly, you will need to get yourself familiar with the rules guiding wholesaling deals, along with the kind of contracts used.

If you are someone who is outgoing and loves to create a new connection and is passionate about real estate, then wholesaling may be ideal for you. After you have properly educated yourself on the intricacies of wholesaling real estate, you will be able to further determine if it is the right form of investment for you or not. As stated above, there are some areas of concern when it comes to this form of investment. First, you need to invest a lot of time to look for distressed properties, along with buyers that will be willing to buy these properties. Nonetheless, if you feel you can put in all of the work involved, and possess the right skills, then it is an investment strategy with immense rewards.

Calculating your Wholesale Profit

If you want to be successful in wholesaling real estate, you need to learn to run your numbers properly. This will help you point out the part of the returns that is your profit. For everyone who invests in a business, profit is the primary goal, and real estate is no different. You need to understand other numbers like ARV and the costs of renovation to determine your profit accurately.

Furthermore, the deal has to be beneficial to all of the parties involved. Simply put, they both need to make returns from the deal. The equation below can make certain that you get a wholesale settlement of no less than $2,000 from every deal you venture into:

Estimated Repair Costs + Contract + $2,000 Wholesale Fee< ARV.

In most instances, buyers need a profit margin of not less than 15% from the deal. The capacity to determine the amount of money you earn from a deal is one of the goals of wholesaling. To make money, its best to purchase real estate at a price which is below the market value. This way, you can sell it to buyers for more than the amount you spent on purchase, and whoever purchases the property from you should still be able to make a profit if they decide to sell. If wholesale does not seem appealing to you, and instead want something more challenging, home rehab or fix and flip may be ideal for you. We will delve into this in the chapter to follow.

Chapter 8: Fix and Flip/Home Rehab

Rehabbing or fix and flip is one of the most expensive projects you can carry on as a real estate investor. It requires a lot of work and can pose a challenge even to experienced investors. If you are just starting, it is even more challenging; however, if you can pull through it, the rewards are outstanding. This form of investment has to do with the purchase of a property, doing repairs, and selling it for a price that covers all the work done.

The rehabbing process is one that needs a lot of time to get around. It also requires one who is very detailed, as forgetting to do even minor repairs can cause you problems down the road. To do a rehab project the right way, you need working capital and some experience. This is not a venture an investor can start without making detailed plans or at least understanding what he or she is getting into. If not done the right way, this is a venture that can lead one to financial ruins; however, the returns are worth it if you take all the right steps.

Knowing this, we will be covering the pros and cons of rehabbing property, and steps to ensure your home rehab project is successful.

Home Rehab: What is it?

In its basic form, it has to do with enhancing a property so it can have a higher market value. When this process is appropriately carried out on a property, it can change its condition from terrible to average or inhabitable, and in other cases perfect. Rehabbing homes is done without making core changes to the basic structure of the home.

Before you start investing in real estate rehab, you need to understand everything involved in a home rehab project. You need to understand all of the strategies available at your disposal to make a profit, and the right amount of cash to invest in the project. Rehabbing can quickly become expensive if you don't do your numbers right, and if the price of a home is too high, you may not be able to get it off the market fast.

Before moving on with a real estate rehab, investors have to comprehend all that is involved in rehabbing. The first thing every investor has to know is that rehabbing is in three categories. There are fix and flip, rental rehab, and personal rehab. Investors have to understand this, as these different approaches will have a significant effect on profit and the amount that is put into financing the project. Now that you have an idea of what it is, below are some of the major benefits, and limitations, of this method of investment.

Advantages of Flipping Properties

Investors can enjoy multiple benefits when they flip properties. Some of these include:

- **Quick profit**: In comparison to holding a property for a few years and hoping the market value will rise naturally, home rehabbing offers a faster ROI.

- **You gain experience**: Flipping houses offers you expertise in various areas. First, you get more experience in the process of renovation and construction. These can be useful to you later down the road. Also, you will gain insight into what to watch out for in the real estate market close to you, and also learn how to do negotiations with vendors and sellers. All of these are vital life skills that can help in other areas.

- **Grow your network**: By delving into the business of flipping houses, you will be able to build a network of professionals. All of these professionals will be of use to you later in the future, and they range from insurance brokers, to real estate agents, other investors, and so on.

Drawbacks of Flipping Properties

- **You can lose money:** It is possible to lose cash instead of making returns, especially if you fail to do your due diligence, or overspend during the process. There is a range of factors that could lead to you losing money ranging from unforeseen expenses, taxes, stamp duty, among many others.

- **Holding costs**: Sometimes, a property may take longer than you projected to sell, and due to this, the cost of maintenance rises. As the owner of the property, you will have to pay all of these costs, and they can weigh on your profit down the line.

- **It is stressful**: The home rehabbing process is not an easy one. It can be time-consuming to find a property below market value, determine the purchase cost, cost of repairs, and locate prospective buyers.

Now that you know the benefits and drawbacks of this form of real estate investment, below is a step by step guide for completing a home rehab project.

Steps in Home Rehabbing

Do Your Research

Some markets are more ideal for flipping homes than others. If you have an available budget of $30,000 to work with, it will certainly not be a great idea to head into markets where prices of homes begin at $700,000. Even with financing, it may be impossible to cover the huge gap.

The lower the amount of cash you have at your disposal, the lower the cost of homes you can work with. How much do you have at your disposal? What are the best markets for you to flip? What types of homes are people purchasing presently?

Your goal as a rehabber is to sell a home fast, so you need to do comprehensive research. Doing this will ensure you don't make the wrong move and end up with an investment that is not profitable.

Develop Your Business Plan and Budget

As an investor in real estate, you are running a business, and as such, you need to put a business plan in place. It does not have to be extremely complex but should at least come with a timeline, budget, and scope of work.

How much do you not want to exceed? How much do you have on ground to invest? Do you have enough money to sort our renovation draws till the lender refunds you? How much time are you willing to spend on the project? When would you like to sell the property?

Answering all of these questions will further put you in the right direction and ensure your project is seamless.

Get Financing in Advance

It can be very frustrating to make an offer, get the approval, and realize you don't have the funding in place to see it through. This is how good deals are lost, which is why it is a wise decision to get your finances in place even before you make an offer on any home.

There are lots of avenues to get financing, which we discussed earlier in chapter 5. Choose one that works for you before you make an offer, and get your finances ready before you need them.

Find the Right Contractors

Similar to finance, you want to start your search for a contractor before you need one. You can develop your relationship with them way before you purchase your first rehab property. The best step is to start requesting quotes the instant you have gotten a property under contract. To be on the safe side, it could be before.

A great part of house flipping is getting your team of contractors and other vital experts together, which we have covered extensively in earlier chapters. Unless you plan on doing all of the work on your own, which is very unlikely if you are working on a large project, you need to get contractors and other professionals in place. All of these experts are vital to the success of your home rehab project.

Locate a Property to Flip

Learning to find suitable properties to flip is also of significant importance. This means you have to purchase a home below the market value and have enough left to cover all of your expenses. Some of the expenses include realtor fees, renovation expenses, holding costs, the cost for your work, etc.

There are a variety of ways to find good deals which we have discussed earlier in chapter 4. Pick a method you find suitable and get a great house flipping deal. To find a good deal, you need to have a lot of patience. It has a lot to do with numbers, and to find a deal, you may need to check out numerous properties before you find the ideal one. However, once you find the right property, all of the efforts will be worth it.

It may be tempting just to make do with what you find and go beyond your budget. But, do your best to stay on course. If your numbers do not add up, it is better for you in the long run to continue your search.

Purchase the Property

After you have found a good deal and gotten approval for your contract, the real work starts. Get in touch with your chosen lender to begin the process of payment. This usually takes a while and is dependent on the kind of lender you choose.

Before this is finalized, get a home inspector to check out the home. These professionals carry out detailed inspections on the property and may spot things that you missed. If you are just starting, it is ideal to go with homes that need only a small amount of repairs. Ensure there is no major repair to be done, and every part of the property is sound.

After you have gotten confirmation that everything is fine, contact a few contractors to get your quotes for repairs. Go through each of them and pick the one you are comfortable with for a final conversation. If your gut agrees with your choice, get them to begin work on the project as soon as possible.

Rehab

After choosing a contractor, it is time to begin work on your project. When it comes to a house rehab, time is of the essence, as your goal should be to dispose of the property fast. For every day you hold onto the property, it means an extra day of paying carrying costs ranging from insurance, taxes, utilities, and so on. All of these can quickly accumulate and eat deep into your projected profit.

This means you want to complete the renovations as fast as you can so you can dispose of the property, settle your loan, and get rewards for all your effort. However, even though you plan to complete a project fast, ensure you learn to spot exaggerated estimates on completion from contactors. Plan for delays and if you have not worked with a contractor beforehand, contact their past clients to determine first-hand if the contractor is reliable or not. This will save you a lot of time and stress down the road.

Sell the Property

This is usually the least complex phase of the process. Your realtor handles most of this, so you want to make sure that you get the services of a professional realtor in your market. All realtors do not come with the same level of skill; neither do they all have the same level of experience. You are on the clock, so the best bet is to go with a realtor with expertise in your market if you want the property to be sold fast.

You can also request that the realtor gives you their professional expertise on prices. However, you should have done your numbers beforehand, and you should only go with prices that you believe will be profitable to you and the efforts you put into the property.

A lot of investors who venture into home rehabbing for the first time often work under the assumption that getting a realtor's license will ease things. This is true to some extent, but you do pay for it with your time and money. Taking the course and the licensing exam does not come cheap. You will also need money to become a member of a brokerage team.

As a first-timer, this can cost a lot of cash you don't necessarily have. So when doing your initial home rehab projects, ensure you collaborate with an experienced realtor. If you then find out flipping homes is something you enjoy doing, then you can take steps to get your real estate license.

If you would rather instead go with an option that offers you a long term investment, there are also other options available to you. One of them is to invest in rental properties, which we will take a more in-depth look at in the next chapter.

Chapter 9: Rental Property Investment

For many investors, a great way to diversify their portfolio is to invest in rental properties which provide long term profit. This is where buy and hold properties come into play, as they can provide you with both short and long term returns. You will be learning about all of the vital areas regarding this form of investment in this chapter. First, a look at what rental real estate means.

Rental Real Estate: What Is It?

This a long-term real estate investing strategy. To do this, investors purchase properties and hold them for a period. The investor may hold on to it until the market value rises before selling, but will usually rent it out to get financing.

It is a kind of investment where investors hope to get income from rent event month, as well as future property appreciation. This form of investment is not as complicated and stressful as home rehabbing, as you don't need to have any prior experience to benefit from this. If you don't want to do any of the work, you can get the services of an expert to aid you in the management of the property. This form of investment is great for newbies in the business of real estate. Knowing this, let us take a look at some of the other benefits and limitations of investing in these kinds of properties.

Benefits of Investing in Rentals

- **Long term revenue**: With rental properties, you get a consistent stream of income which you can use to cover running costs, or increase your wealth. Furthermore, in other forms of investment, the instant you have issues with your health, your investment tends to suffer. However, having a rental property ensures you keep earning income even if you are unable to work or are in bad shape health-wise.

- **It is a source of passive income**: If you hire an expert to handle the rental property for you, it can be a consistent source of passive income. You can even benefit from these properties alongside a full-time job.

- **It is an excellent way to keep a property**: Instead of selling off your home in a bad market, or when you relocate, renting it out is an excellent way of holding on to it. You do this while it also makes money for you.

- **Tenants are always available:** There will always be people to rent homes. People move to new cities every day, and this means you can never get a shortage of tenants for your property. Even when there is an economic downturn, people will always require a roof over their heads.

- You can use the income from tenants to clear up mortgages

- You can claim a reasonable amount of tax deductions due to your rentals.

Drawbacks of Investing in Rentals

- **You spend more on maintenance in comparison to a property you live in**: This is because people do not treat rented properties the same way as they would their home.

- **There are instances you fall into the trap of getting a frustrating tenant**: These tenants will forge stories to get past your screening process, and may have the worst credit scores you can find. They may be unable to pay, which results in you losing income and going through the stress of an eviction.

- **If you own a rental, at some point, you may have a lawsuit on your hands**: This is the case even if it was not your fault. Rents can also cost you more money in terms of creating legal documents, legal fees, and so on. Similar to other forms of business, this is something you cannot avoid.

- **There are moments when having a rental can be very stressful**: This is mainly the case when you have a shortage of tenants. This stress can find its way to your personal life and hamper your overall well-being. However, this is a situation you can quickly correct by hiring a property manager, and free yourself from all of the hassles involved.

Having covered the benefits and drawbacks of having a rental, we will look into the steps involved in investing in these kinds of properties below.

How to Invest in Rental Properties

Do Comprehensive Research Before You Buy

Similar to other forms of investment, this is a step that you cannot ignore. The moment you decide to buy a rental property, it is vital that you know what you are getting yourself into. Knowing this, you have to do some research on the following areas:

- The kind of rental investment property to buy

- The peak amount you are willing to spend

- The type of neighborhood you want to purchase the property in

- The average price of rent in that neighborhood

- The rate of return you would like to earn from your investment

Create a Plan

Once you have adequately armed yourself with information from your research, you can begin to develop a plan, alongside the criteria you want to utilize. It is crucial for you to write out your plans and objectives, so you can check them out as frequently as you need to. If you want properties within the prices of $100,000 to $200,000, it is pointless to be carried away with properties that have the latest modern facilities ranging from $300,000 and above. By putting down your plan and your criteria, it will ensure you don't deviate from it.

Get Your Finances in Order

Many investors make the error of getting funding together after they have found a property. This is a bad idea, as you may find a good deal only to realize you are unable to afford it. If you head into a store to shop for groceries, you need to have a way to pay before making the purchase. You don't pick up your groceries before thinking about a means to pay.

This concept applies to rental real estate as well; it is ideal to have a plan in place with a lender or bank in advance on the amount of downpayment you can make. As we have stated earlier in chapter 5, there are a variety of options for financing you can choose from.

Begin Your Search for a Rental Property You Can Buy

Now that you have gotten your finances in order, the next step is to search for a rental property to purchase. You can begin your search by checking out the listings on the local MLS. You can also refer to the earlier chapter on how to find great deals to locate a suitable method for you.

If you would instead go with a website, there are numerous options available to you which consist of:

- Redfin.com
- Trulia.com
- Realtor.com
- Zillow.com

On the downside, you can find the same listings as you would on the MLS on these sites, but you may not see all of the information you need. For this reason, it is crucial to reach out to a local real estate agent you trust, and you can rely on, to aid you in getting all the information you need.

To further assist you, it is ideal to find agents who have

experience in working with rental real estate investors. This will save you from the hassle of having to explain all of your requirements from scratch. By going with one that has the experience, your work is less difficult, as they understand all that is required in a rental property. Also, its best to let your agent know what you desire in a property, as this will aid them in pointing out the best options for you.

Make the Seller an Offer

After you have located a suitable property to buy, and you have taken a look around the property, the next thing you need to do is make the seller an offer. For this to successfully take place, you need to get your agent to fill out paperwork which is based on your specifications, and then make your offer to the selling agent. Next, the selling agent gives the offer to the seller, which then ensures negotiations can start.

Be sure to remain in line with your allocated budget. You need to logically calculate the amount of cash you are willing to spend. You need to make sure that you don't let emotions rule you. The numbers should be the only thing important to you. You have to be ready to leave the deal and walk away, as this will give you an upper hand during the process of negotiation. If you can't reach an agreed price, your best bet is to walk away.

However, when making an offer, you need to look into a lot of other things apart from price. Some of these include:

- Inspection contingency
- Closing date
- Financing contingency
- Seller financial concessions

All of these factors are crucial, and you have to ponder on them to determine if they will be included in your offer or not. Be sure to speak with the real estate agent as regards the crucial areas of your offer. The instant you have reached an agreement, and the seller has appended his or her signature on the contract, you have now established what is called mutual acceptance.

Do Your Due Diligence

After you have reached a price and a closing date has been put in place, you can now begin your due diligence. To do this, you can call on a professional inspector to help you inspect the chosen property. This professional will help you search for defects in the property, which can help you get a better purchase value later on. If something is noted, you can renegotiate the terms of the deal.

Getting the Services of a Property Manager

It is possible to manage your rental property by yourself after you have made a purchase, but you can also get the services of a professional property manager. This is not compulsory, but if you are not going to be available to manage your property, you may need the help of a property manager. Still, the same may be the case even if you reside not far from your rental. Perhaps you have other obligations that take up most of your time which make it impossible to manage the property yourself. Or maybe you just don't want to go through the stress of heading out any time of the day to deal with emergencies that may arise on the property.

While it may save you a lot of time and stress to get the services of a property manager, it also implies that you will have to let go of the daily running of your rental project. By getting the services of a great property manager, you can free yourself from a considerable part of the responsibilities associated with managing your rental, which then transforms your lease to an investment that brings you passive income. Also, great property managers may have developed excellent relationships with vendors, which can be beneficial to you and your property in the long run.

If you get the services of a property manager, its best to come to an agreement as regards the selection criteria of tenants. This is because the property manager is not an actual homeowner, and may not deal with things in the same manner as the investor, or landlord.

Is Investing in Rental Properties a Wise Decision?

If you are an investor who has the capacity to remain focused on his or her business and financial goals, then this form of investment is ideal for you. When you do it the right way, investing in a buy and hold real estate can bring you a massive amount of returns. What's more, you can tailor them to your requirements, and even get the services of a professional property manager to take the bulk work of supervising operations off you. This is undoubtedly a smart investment decision, so long as you know what you are getting into and have an interest in earning long-term income.

Chapter 10: Making Offers in Real Estate

After you have found a property you like, you will want to make an offer to the seller. However, for new investors, this process can seem like a scary one, as it involves a lot of phases. After creating an offer, you will need to negotiate and anticipate counter offers from sellers. All of these can seem daunting, especially if you don't know how to go about it. In this chapter, we will be looking into some helpful strategies that can help ensure your first one is as seamless as possible.

Develop an Amazing Offer

When making an offer on a property you want to invest in, you need to make sure that the offer is the best it can be. This is vital because your goal is to win the bid. The tips below can be of help when putting your offer together.

Run an Analysis of the Market

Before you place an offer, get the services of a contractor or agent to help you with a comparative market analysis. With this, you will get a perspective on your local real estate market behavior. This is a crucial step which becomes particularly more crucial for properties that have been on the market for a while. Also, a comparative market analysis will give you insights on whether or not a property has been overvalued. For instance, if the analysis lets you know that a property is meant to be in the lines of $250,000 - $300,000, but is valued at $400,00, you will have enough leverage to negotiate better prices for yourself. The reverse is also applicable, as a comparative analysis makes certain that you don't bid way below the actual property range in your offer. All of these give you the opportunity of making the winning offer.

Monitor Market Indicators

Also, from what the market analysis shows you, another equally important area is the market in the neighborhood you want to purchase your property. You need to find out how long properties in the region stay on the market, as this will give you insight into the state of the real estate market there.

This will reveal to you if it is a seller's market, buyer's market, or neither. Properties in a seller's market don't stay so long on the market in comparison to a seller's market. In essence, properties have a faster sell rate in a seller's market.

When crafting your offer, you must note the present local demand. You need to ensure it is not so far off from the other offers the seller is getting on his or her property. If the property of a seller has been recently listed on the market, he or she will not be as willing to accept lower bids, in contrast with a seller whose property has been on the market for a while. Properties in markets with plenty of competition can attract high bids even if they have not spent very long on the market. Always reach out to your realtor for help before you make any move in real estate. This is necessary because even the smallest error can lead to substantial financial losses.

Determine the Motivation of the Seller

If you understand why the seller is motivated to sell his or her property, you will be a step ahead of the other bidders. Some homeowners want to dispose of their properties as fast as possible. If you know the reason behind this, you can use it as leverage to get a better price and terms. Various sellers are motivated to sell for numerous reasons, and they are known as motivated sellers. Most times, they are eager to accept prices which are much lower than the value of their property. This is most prominent in a buyer's market. However, some sellers are in no rush and will be more than willing to hold on till they get a good offer. This makes it necessary to understand the seller's motivation.

Find out About the Other Offers on the Property

Not every seller will be obligated to let you know about the different offers on the property. Offers will be placed on record only if a seller accepts it. To find out the competing offers, you may have to get the services of a professional agent or contractor. If your agent completes the research and learns that there have already been lots of offers for the property, send in your offer quickly. Make certain that the offer you send is more seller-friendly if you believe there is more competition. This way, your offer can stand out from the others and probably be given more priority.

Apply for a Pre-approval Letter

If you are using financing for your deal, make certain that you get a pre-approval letter from your bank. This will act as an assurance that you can get as much as the asking price of the property from your lender or bank as a loan or mortgage. Once you send in your request, a pre-approval letter will be granted to you by your loan officer. To obtain this letter, you will need to go through a credit check or provide precise information on your assets and earnings.

You need to note that a pre-approval letter is not the same as loan approval. The role of a pre-approval letter is to stand as a form of assurance that your loan will eventually be approved. Many sellers may not take offers that don't come with an attached pre-approval letter seriously. However, if you are planning to complete the deal in cash, you don't need a pre-approval letter since there is no financing involved.

Make a Larger Downpayment

When it comes to purchasing a property, your deal will be more appealing to the seller if you pay a downpayment. The reason for this is that there is a lower possibility of smaller loans not falling through due to problems with financing.

Let an Attorney Evaluate Your Offer

As a property buyer, it will be necessary for you to sign a purchase offer. This is an important legal document, and even if no law recommends that an attorney is present while signing this document, it's best to come with an attorney. This way, you protect yourself from being defrauded.

Engaging in Negotiations

Negotiations are a vital part of purchasing a property. You need to negotiate with the seller to get a better deal. With the right negotiation strategy, the buyer will be more likely to go with your offer over the others he or she has received. However, you need to understand the kind of negotiation strategy that would be ideal for you.

In real estate investment, there are two forms of negotiations which are open negotiations and sealed beading. The first step before you head into any negotiation is to determine your budget, as well as the highest you can afford to go while bidding. It is also essential that you include the additional charges that come with buying a property.

Bidding Strategies

The bidding strategy you choose to go with has a lot to do with the bidding process. Below is a guide on how to go about bidding:

Open negotiation: Begin with a low bid

When it comes to negotiation, it is a norm for sellers to put a higher value on a product or service they are about to sell. This is the case even in real estate. When you want to negotiate, always begin with a low bid. Typically, individuals start bids by offering 6 – 15% less than the property's asking price.

Keep your cool

While bidding, remember to stay polite and calm during the entire process. If you let yourself lose your cool, it can result in frustration. Being frustrated during bids can quickly make a negotiation go in the wrong direction.

Play hard to get

Even as you make an effort to remain realistic while bidding, it is essential to play hard to get during a period of negotiation. If the seller is one who is very eager to sell, and even seems desperate, you can make it work for you. Behave as if you have no interest due to the asking price, and if the seller is desperate enough, he or she will tone it down to align with your offer.

Contact the seller directly

Sometimes, it is best to contact the seller by yourself. Making use of intermediaries may prevent you from spotting signs that you could have used to your benefit during negotiations. However, it can be a challenge to deal with sellers directly, but if it is something you can handle, it is worth the try.

Sealed bids

Sealed bids have to do with sending you offers via an agent, in a sealed envelope. The agent is tasked with communicating the offers to the seller. When the seller gets the offer, he or she goes with the highest bid. The aim of sealed bids is to draw in the highest price, as buyers put in their best offers to ensure they do better than the competitors.

In a highly competitive market, sealed bids are the typical process for negotiations. It is very easy to get carried away during sealed bidding, so you need to make sure you don't go beyond your set budget. If you do this, your mortgage may be unable to cover beyond the asking price.

Holding Deposits

There are markets where sellers ask buyers to add some cash when sending in their offers. In real estate investment, it is known as holding deposits. This is a way of making sure that the buyers are genuinely interested in the purchase of a property.

Holding deposits are not required by all sellers, but if the market is very competitive one, then it may be a requirement.

Some of the kinds of holding requests include:

- Refundable holding deposits
- Non-refundable holding deposits

As one who wants to purchase a property, it is not recommended that you go with a non-refundable holding deposit. This is because, if the seller chooses not to sell to you, he or she is allowed by law to pick someone else, while holding on to your deposit.

In most instances, after you have turned in your offer, you need to be ready to get a counteroffer from the seller.

Seller Counteroffers and Responses

Usually, the seller responds to purchase offers when the consideration window ends. If the seller does not find your offer good enough, he or she can reject or disregard the offer. However, you are most likely going to get a counteroffer which can come in the following ways:

- **The seller accepts the terms**: If your offer is satisfactory to the seller, he or she agrees with the offer, and you both get into an agreement.
- **The seller rejects the terms**: If the seller feels your

offer is not satisfactory, he or she is legally allowed to disregard it.

Send a Counteroffer: If the seller finds the offer sent by a buyer satisfactory, but not satisfying enough, he or she can alter a few areas of the offer. Then, when the seller is through making changes, he or she signs and sends it back to the buyer. This is known as a counteroffer, and as a buyer, you are allowed to alter the offer and send back to the seller or accept it. This can go on till the negotiation is canceled by one of the parties, or an agreement is reached.

After you have made an offer for the property, the next step will be to do your due diligence. The next chapter will teach you how to go about doing this.

Chapter 10: Doing Your Due Diligence

Due diligence is something you must not overlook when it comes to real estate. It has to do with the research a real estate investor carries out before buying a property. The goal of due diligence is to ensure that there are no problem areas in a property before purchase. Make sure that you do a comprehensive inspection of the property after an appraisal.

There is a lot more involved in due diligence, which is not something you can point out at just a glance. You need to consider an array of factors that have an impact on the amount you can earn from a property. In this chapter, we will be taking a look at some due diligence tips which will ensure you get the best out of your investment.

Tasks Involved in Due Diligence

Due diligence helps you make sure that the property you purchase aligns with your numbers. Below are a few things you need to do before you complete a property purchase.

Do Your Research

Before you sign any document, ensure you carefully go through it in detail. Do a physical evaluation of the property, and analyze the cost of insurance. Check out the area's market trends and values and budget for unforeseen expenses. You need to be as detailed as you can all through this process to ensure you can get the most profit from the property if you do decide to buy. Make an exhaustive list of all the benefits and drawbacks of the property you are planning to invest in, and don't forget to analyze every area, even the ones that seem insignificant.

If you requested financing, ensure you do an appraisal, as it underlines a property's value. If you request a mortgage, an appraisal will also be required by banks and other lenders to make sure that the property is worth the value placed on it. If the property fails to align with the value once the evaluation is done, you won't get approval for the loan. However, this can be reversed if the seller agrees to cut down on the property's price to what has been evaluated as the actual value.

To inspect the property, you will require the services of a property inspector, alongside a skilled appraiser. The appraiser will be of help when it has to do with the needed enhancements, the size of the property, where the property is located, and so on. The appraiser will also do a comparative analysis of other properties similar to what you want to purchase in the area. With an appraisal, you can make certain that you don't pay more than a property's market value.

Do a Title Search

Before you close on your purchase of a property, do research on the title history. This will aid you in ascertaining the actual property owner before you make a purchase. This is important, as it will ensure you don't have problems with ownership later down the line. If the past owner does some work on the property, and does not make complete payment to the contractors who worked on the property, the owner will have to pay the lien on the property entirely before selling. If you don't know about the lien before you buy a property, you will need to clear off the debt before the title of the property can be cleared.

After you have done a comprehensive check, you need to send in an application for an owner's title insurance to ensure you don't fall into issues that you may not have seen while doing research on the title. Some of the problems could span from undisclosed heirs, the omission of deeds, forgery, recording mistakes, among others. By getting an owner's title insurance, you can safeguard yourself from liens that may arise after closing the deal. Any lien that was not identified which arises, will be sorted out by the insurance company.

Follow the Homeowner's Association Requirements

Before you purchase a townhouse, apartment, single-family apartment, or condo in specific regions, do research on the guidelines and rules put in place by the homeowner's association. When you have uncovered these rules, ensure you go with all of the stated requirements. As a property homeowner, there are strict rules and regulations put in place by the homeowner's association which you need to observe. These rules are put in place and enforced to safeguard the appearance of the neighborhood you are in, alongside its values.

For example, there may be a restriction on parking a recreational vehicle on the driveway. If you fail to go with these rules, you may need to pay a fine. This is why it is of the utmost importance that you go with the laws and regulations put in place by the homeowner's association.

Doing a Property Inspection

Carrying out an inspection on a property you want to purchase is something you can't overlook. This would be your final hurdle to ensure that the property you are trying to purchase is in great shape.

As stated before, it is in your best interest to get the services of a licensed inspector instead of doing it on your own. But you need to understand that there are moments home inspectors may not be perfect and fail to point out specific issues. Inspectors point out the things you need to repair and change, and even though this is very important, this is not all the information you require to make a decision.

There are other areas you may want to take note of as well, which include:

- The amount of water you can find on the property, alongside its quality.

- Make certain that there is no mold in the property.

- Lack of radon, or its existence in the property. This is because radon has been proven to lead to cancer.

- Existence of lead paint for properties developed earlier than 1978. This information is crucial for individuals who have children not above six years of age.

Making Preparations for a Property Inspection

Before the property inspection, there is a collection of things you need to make available. An easy way to do this is to outline all of the aspects of the property that require inspection. Some of the things that should be included in this list should span from:

- Doors and windows

- Exterior paint

- Rain gutters and downspouts

- Power outlets, electrical panel, and light switches

- Porches and balconies

- Walkways and driveways

- Steps, stairs, and railings

- Garage

- Foundation

- Walls, floors, and ceilings

- Roof

- Water heaters, faucets, and plumbing fixtures

- Basement

- Appliances

- Attic space

- Heating, HVAC system, thermostats, and cooling

The inspection lasts for only a few hours, and it is best to make yourself available while this is ongoing. Doing this will provide you with adequate data on the property's shape. Outline all of the vital things, take a few pictures, and ask questions about things you are not satisfied with.

Things Home Inspection Might Not Cover

The comprehensiveness of an inspection may differ based on the inspector. However, most inspectors are mostly interested in the physical features of the home. There are other areas you may need to inspect by yourself, which are:

- Pests that wreck wood such as carpenter ants and termites
- Fireplace and chimney
- Lawn sprinklers
- Floors obscured by carpeting
- Trees and landscape
- Internet and cell service
- Drainage
- Sewer lines
- Equipment for swimming pool
- Rodents, rats, and mice
- Odors

There are numerous considerations when inspecting a property you want to channel your resources into. We will now be looking into the forms of inspections you need to carry out before you buy a property.

Things to Inspect on a Property

Before you purchase a property to invest in, it is vital that you do not overlook inspection. Most lenders will request that you do an inspection before they offer you a loan, and as stated above, a licensed contractor or home inspector can help out with this. This can consist of a comprehensive account on the water heater, kitchen appliances, roof, and so on. The inspector will also offer an outline of all the spotted issues and how serious they are.

After carrying out a detailed inspection, it is not abnormal to spot some critical repairs you need to carry out, which will cost you a little extra. There are instances where the repair estimate will be so excessive that the buyer will have to walk away from the deal and find a more profitable option. This makes it necessary to accommodate cancelations in the buyer agreement after an inspection is finished. Also, you need to secure your cash deposit in the event you walk away from the offer.

Inspection for Wood-destroying Organisms (WDO)

Before you are provided with financing, many lenders will ask for this inspection to be carried out. Through this inspection, you will learn if the property's structure has a presence of wood rot. Various factors lead to wood rot, and some of these include water damage or termites. There is an array of areas you need to inspect which include the garage, interior walls, exterior walls, and so on. If there is a severe case of wood rot on a property, it could hamper the structural integrity of the property. The inspector will let you know how severe the wood rot is, which will help you determine if it is worth the risk.

Radon Gas Inspection

This kind of inspection is not a popular one. However, in the US, this specific gas is prevalent in numerous homes. The Surgeon General and EPA have stated that being exposed to this gas for long periods has been proven to cause multiple deaths each year through lung cancer.

Lead-based Paint Inspection

This is a form of inspection which is required by law for all properties developed in 1978 and before that. If a seller is aware that there is lead-based paint on the exterior or interior of a home, they are bound by law to inform prospective buyers.

Furthermore, it is still required by the buyer to carry out inspections of their own to be on the safe side. Lead-based paint can cause a lot of harm to the health of individuals, and it will require cash to get rid of before the home becomes habitable for individuals. The instant the inspections are over, the following are some of the options available to you:

- Reject the deal

- Go ahead with the offer after you have accepted the way the property is
- Request a better offer

If everything is satisfactory for you, then you can go ahead and sign an agreement with the property's seller. However, if there are minor problems with the property, you can ask to renegotiate the offer before you walk away. For instance, if the issues are small, you can request that the seller fixes them, or takes out the estimated cost of repairing it from the selling price.

The Final Step: Run Your Numbers

After you have obtained all the needed information, the final step will have to do with running your numbers. In addition to your due diligence, this can help you determine if you should go ahead with the offer or walk away.

If after doing your numbers you find out that you can make a profit off property, then you can go ahead with your purchase. But what should you do when your numbers do not add up? Let's find out below.

What Should You Do When the Numbers Are Not Right?

As an investor, you do not want this. But if the numbers are not right after you do your due diligence, the following are the options available to you:

Request a price reduction

This is the first option available to you. Reach out to the seller and inform him or her of the discrepancy noticed in your number and request for contributions from them. If you can prove that you have observed problems that may have an impact on your overall cost, he or she should be willing to offer you a price reduction. In the case of REP deals, the bank will request that you showcase inspection reports or bids from contractors before they can provide a discount.

Reject the deal

If you are unable to get a price reduction, the next step may be to revoke the deal. This may not be satisfactory to all the parties involved, but there is no point investing in a money drainer.

Chapter 11: Common Real Estate Misconceptions

There have been some misconceptions about the real estate industry from time immemorial. These misconceptions are developed from false myths that are passed around from many individuals. Some of these false myths may deter a real estate investor from making the best decision at the right time or even prevent them from investing in the real estate sector at all. Some of these myths may also mislead an investor into investing wrongly and ending up in huge losses. In this chapter, we will be discussing some of these myths below.

Making Money in Real Estate is Very Easy

One of the most popular beliefs in real estate is that making money is quite easy. Even though you can become a millionaire or even billionaire in the real estate industry, you need to know that this is something that does not happen overnight. You have to be sure of what you're doing and have lots of patience.

If you give up too soon because you cannot deal with the many uncertainties that come with the real estate business, then making money will be difficult. To be a successful real estate businessman, you also need to be focused and understand the nitty-gritty of the business. When you do all of this and have enough patience, you'll succeed in the business.

The Best Place to Buy Real Estate is Downtown

Due to the little cost involved in investing in downtown properties, many people assume it's the best place to buy properties. Nevertheless, the cost of renting out properties in downtown is usually lower because of the location. So, there's no best place to invest; the best thing is finding the right property and investing smartly.

You Need a Ton of Money to Start the Business

When people hear the words "real estate investments," what they think is millions and billions. But this isn't right. Even though investing in real estate requires money, the money doesn't have to be a huge sum. You'll come across huge deals, but this doesn't mean you cannot get smaller deals. One popular example of real estate investment that requires a little amount of money is the fix and flip method. Fix and flip means when you buy good properties that need little touches or renovations at lesser prices and sell them at higher rates after the upgrades.

Another popular option is the Buy, Rehab, Rent, Refinance, and Repeat (BRRRR) method, which involves buying a home, rehabilitating it and renting it out. After this, you refinance a similar kind of project and repeat the process. Once you've rented out the apartment, you can then use the money realized to pay off the loan you used to finance the project. When you gain enough experience from either BRRRR or fix and flip, you can easily move on to investing massive sums and getting more profit.

However, the above options may come with lost as some risks come with it. If your calculations were wrong and you end up losing rather than making a profit, then more money will have to be invested in the business to get the desired result. If you're scared of bearing the burden of this unexpected risk, you can get a partner in order to spend less.

Having a Home Should Come First Before Investment

Many people also believe that there's a need for them to have a home before they invest in real estate. This isn't true, as you can invest in a property and live in it. By doing this, you're investing and being a homeowner at the same time. Being a real estate investor requires you to be smart and being a homeowner as well as the occupier is one very smart strategy among a ton of others.

Investing in Real Estate Requires you to Have a License

Another misconception in the real estate industry is that people misconstrue the duties of a real estate agent and real estate investors. A real estate investor does not need a license to operate, but a real estate agent may need one. All that is required is a good knowledge of how the industry works and the willingness to know more. You can learn through constant research and experiences and ask questions when you need clarifications.

Tenants Leave When Rent is Increased

Another erroneous belief is that tenants will disappear when the cost of rent increases. Even though it is necessary to increase the rent when the situation warrants it, tenants may pay the rent and stay rather than leaving. Nonetheless, it is essential to not overdo things by increasing the rent every year. It's better to increase it over a few years in order to make it easier for the tenant to pay. So, when you increase the rent based on the current market value of your property after a few years, your tenant will find it reasonable and pay. With this, you'll be able to maximize profit.

You Can Earn Passively by Investing in Real Estate

Some people believe that real estate can give you passive income. Although this is not entirely wrong, if the only reason you're investing in real estate is to earn passively, you wouldn't make enough profit. Also, you need to put in the required effort first-hand before you can begin to make a passive income from real estate.

The more effort you put in, and the more coordinated you are, the more you earn from real estate investment. Before and after you buy a property, you need to put things in order and take the necessary steps.

You Should be a Homeowner Before Investing in Rental Properties

This is yet another false myth you hear in the real estate industry. You can invest in a rental property without being a homeowner. The advantage is enormous, as you gain more if you do your research and do things the right way.

You Must Always Make a Huge Profit

Many people believe that investing in real estate requires you to always make plenty of profit. This erroneous belief makes people think that they should make money as soon as they invest in a property. But, every investment needs to grow before it can yield profit, and the real estate industry is not left out. Being a real estate investor requires lots of patience before the profits come along.

Your Investment Should be Close to Where You Live

Some people believe it's best to invest in properties that are closer to where you live, but this isn't always true. Investing in properties close to your home is nice, but if you find a great deal far from home, nothing stops you from investing in such property. You may be concerned about not having a good knowledge of the locality, but you can ask real estate agents and investors around the region or search online for necessary information.

You Need to Have Connections to Invest

Having connections is not as important as having a great team that will ensure the success of your project. The different professionals that make up your team will guide you and provide you with the necessary information you need to succeed and the required experience. So, you do not need to have secure connections to be a successful real estate investor.

You Need Luck to Make a Substantial Profit

Sometimes you need luck to make it in the industry, but it's never a determinant of how successful you'll become. As long as you do your due diligence, you're one step ahead and closer to being successful. The smarter the work you put in, the higher your chances of making a huge profit.

You Can Make Money While You Sleep Once You Own Lots of Properties

While this is true to some extent, it won't be possible if you do not put in the needed effort. You can have lots of properties and run at a loss. It all boils down to how diligent and willing you are. If you're willing to let it work, you'll sure try your best to make it work. You can't possibly do things wrong and expect to make a profit while you sleep.

Conclusion

Congratulations! You have gotten to the end of this fantastic journey. This says a lot about how serious you are about becoming a real investor, and you've made a good choice by trying to know more from this book. All that you've read will help you succeed in the real estate industry. The level of commitment and interest you have shown so far will help you throughout your journey into the real estate world. You'll come across various challenges and difficulties, but your determination will get you going. You'll also be exposed to some risks, but you'll scale through since you're well prepared for them.

Ensure you come up with a good plan and make necessary findings before buying any property to avoid problems later. Challenges will always come up, but they will be minimal when you do your due diligence.

If you're a first-time investor, do not rely on your knowledge alone, as this can be disastrous in the long run. Work with the right set of people to save yourself from various problems that may arise along the line. Do all you can to get good hands and employ the help of professionals. As you work with them and invest in more and more properties, you'll have a better understanding of what works and what doesn't work.

Read, understand, and digest the information in this book and repeat the process. Apply it in your real estate experiences and see yourself succeed in this beautiful world of opportunities.

See you at the top of your real estate career!

www.ingramcontent.com/pod-product-compliance
Lightning Source LLC
Chambersburg PA
CBHW070648220526

45466CB00001B/344